LIBRA
2000

With love to Bill, Jean, Rob and Shani

This is the third year that I've written these books and it's about time I thanked all the people who help me to put them together. I have worked with some of them since the beginning of the books, and others have only recently started lending me their help, but I am immensely grateful to them all. So thank you, Nova Jayne Heath, Nicola Chalton, Nick Robinson and everyone else at Robinson Publishing for being such a great team to work with. Thanks to Chelsey Fox for all her agenting skills. And a huge thank you to Annie Lionnet and Jamie Macphail for their tireless work.

LIBRA
2000

Jane Struthers

First published in 1999 by Parragon

Parragon
Queen Street House
4 Queen Street
Bath BA1 1HE
UK

Produced by Magpie Books, an imprint of
Robinson Publishing Ltd, London

© Jane Struthers 1999

Illustrations courtesy of Slatter-Anderson, London

ISBN 0 75252 896 3

A copy of the British Library Cataloguing-in-Publication Data
is available from the British Library

Printed and bound in the EC

CONTENTS

Dates for 2000

Libra 22 September – 22 October

Scorpio 23 October – 21 November

Sagittarius 22 November – 20 December

Capricorn 21 December – 19 January

Aquarius 20 January – 18 February

Pisces 19 February – 19 March

Aries 20 March – 18 April

Taurus 19 April – 19 May

Gemini 20 May – 20 June

Cancer 21 June – 21 July

Leo 22 July – 21 August

Virgo 22 August – 21 September

YOUR LIBRA SUN SIGN

This chapter is all about your Sun sign. I'm going to describe your general personality, as well as the way you react in relationships, how you handle money, what your health is like and which careers suit you. But before I do all that, I want to explain what a Sun sign is. It's the sign that the Sun occupied at the time of your birth. Every year, the Sun moves through the sky, spending an average of 30 days in each of the signs. You're a Libran, which means that you were born when the Sun was moving through the sign of Libra. It's the same as saying that Libra is your star sign, but astrologers prefer to use the term 'Sun sign' because it's more accurate.

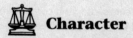 **Character**

You stand head and shoulders above the rest of the zodiac when it comes to charm and diplomacy. You have plenty of both, and as a result Librans are the natural peace-makers and diplomats of the zodiac.

Libra is the sign of balance and harmony, and you strive to have both of these qualities in your life. This means that you're always trying to find the happy medium and to strike the right note in situations.

There's something wonderfully calming and relaxing about you, even if you're a knot of tension inside. Part of this is your ability to put other people first and yourself second, so whenever you talk to someone you let them feel that they're the only person in the world as far as you're concerned. Perhaps this is where your reputation as a flirt comes from, because you're able to direct these megawatts of charm to whoever you happen to be talking to. It might be your one true love or it could be the postman, but they'll end the conversation feeling a lot better than when they started it. You've got your ruler, Venus, to thank for this, and also for the fact that tradition says Libra is the best-looking sign of all. And it's true in your case!

Libra is one of the three Air signs, which means you operate on an intellectual level. The combination of Venus, who makes you reluctant to hurt people, and your intellectual element of Air, means you always see at least two sides to every story and would rather sit on the fence than make up your mind. No wonder you're known for your indecision!

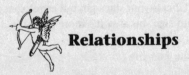 **Relationships**

This is where you come into your own because your sign rules partnerships of all kinds. You feel like a fish out of water if you have to spend too long on your own. Your charm makes you immensely popular and you can be extremely affectionate, loving and romantic. People find it hard to resist you. It's very difficult for you to cope with loneliness, so you may prefer to be in an unhappy relationship than no relationship at all.

It's extremely easy for other people to hurt your feelings, although you're reluctant to let anyone know how bad you feel. Some Librans can fall in love with love, perhaps because they're so keen to find a soulmate. You're also very idealistic and only tend to see the good in other people. When you do find a special someone, you tend to put them on a pedestal, looking up to them and inevitably feeling crushed and disappointed when they reveal that they're human after all. Sadly, there are times when someone hurts you but you come straight back for more – it's as if you can't learn from the experience.

 **Money**

You love luxury and the good things in life, so it's no surprise that money has a habit of slipping through your fingers. There are so many things to spend it on, and so many temptations, that your biggest worry is deciding what to buy first. The arrival of your second worry usually coincides with that of your credit card or bank statement, but that's another story and one that you're probably all too familiar with. (And it's not helped by your inbuilt reluctance to confront anything unpleasant or ugly, so you'll tell yourself that things are a lot better than you imagine provided you can bring yourself to open the envelope in the first place.)

You enjoy spending your money on items that will bring pleasure to you and your loved ones, especially if you can give them a treat. However, you must avoid any tendency to lavish presents on people because you want to buy their affection rather than because you want to make them happy. Far better to be honest about what you want, and to trust that people will love you for yourself rather than your spending power.

Health

Librans are very healthy on the whole, but your love of the good life makes it easy for you to put on weight. It's one of the disadvantages of being ruled by Venus – she gives you good looks, immense charm and a beautiful voice, but also makes you prone to piling on the pounds. Mind you, the fact that you have a sweet tooth and enjoy eating rich foods won't help much, either. The best antidote to all this is plenty of exercise but, unless you're a very unusual Libran, the thought of this doesn't exactly make you want to leap off the sofa and put on your jogging kit. Try to find a sport or activity that truly appeals to you, especially if you can combine it with a social activity, otherwise you'll never stick with it. You should also make sure you exercise regularly and steadily – don't follow a long period of inactivity with a hectic few hours in the gym.

The area of the body ruled by Libra is the kidneys, so you need to keep an eye on any irregularities that could cause headaches or back ache. If your social life involves drinking a lot of alcohol, try to combat its effects by drinking lots of water and fruit juices to give your kidneys a chance to flush out all those toxins.

Career

If you're a typical Libran you enjoy the high life, which means you need plenty of money to be able to afford it. As a result, you need a good job that brings in lots of cash and, preferably, a few perks such an expense account (which you'll enjoy using) and an attractive car.

It's important that you work in a comfortable and pleasant environment – anything too Spartan or tacky will turn you off fast. It's also important for you to feel happy with your colleagues, because you'll hate coming into work if there's a tense atmosphere between you or the threat of a row always hangs in the air. You can't bear workmates who are nit-pickers or troublemakers. They may even make you feel ill.

Ideally, you should be part of a team. Working on your own doesn't suit you, partly because you quickly feel lonely and partly because it can be difficult to motivate yourself sometimes. Any job that makes the most of your charm and intellect will bring out the best in you, but professions that are particularly good for Librans include diplomacy, fashion, beauty and music.

MERCURY AND YOUR COMMUNICATIONS

Where would we be without Mercury? This tiny planet rules everything connected with our communications, from the way we speak to the way we get about. The position of Mercury in your birth chart describes how fast or how slow you absorb information, the sorts of things you talk about, the way you communicate with other people and how much nervous energy you have.

Mercury is an important part of everyone's birth chart, but it has extra meaning for Geminis and Virgos because both these signs are ruled by Mercury.

Mercury is the closest planet to the Sun in the solar system, and its orbit lies between the Earth and the Sun. In fact, it is never more than 28 degrees away from the Sun. Mercury is one of the smallest known planets in the solar system, but it makes up in speed what it lacks in size. It whizzes around the Sun at about 108,000 miles an hour, to avoid being sucked into the Sun's fiery mass.

If you've always wondered how astrology works, here's a brief explanation. Your horoscope (a map of the planets' positions at the time of your birth) is divided up into twelve sections, known as 'houses'. Each one represents a different area of your life, and together they cover every aspect of our experiences on Earth. As Mercury moves around the heavens each year it progresses through each house in turn, affecting a particular part of your life, such as your health or career. If you plot its progress through your own chart, you'll be able to make the most of Mercury's influence in 2000. That way, you'll know when it's best to make contact with others and when it's wisest to keep your thoughts to yourself.

Mercury takes just over one year to complete its orbit of the Earth, but during this time it doesn't always travel forwards, it also appears to go backwards. When this happens, it means that, from our vantage point on Earth, Mercury has slowed down to such an extent that it seems to be backtracking through the skies. We call this retrograde motion. When Mercury is travelling forwards, we call it direct motion.

All the planets, with the exception of the Sun and Moon, go retrograde at some point during their orbit of the Earth. A retrograde Mercury is very important because it means that during this time our communications can hit delays and snags. Messages may go missing, letters could get lost in the post, appliances and gadgets can go on the blink. You may also find it hard to make yourself understood. In 2000, there are several periods when Mercury goes retrograde. These are between 21 February and 14 March, 23 June and 17 July, and between 18 October and 8 November. These are all times to keep a close eye on your communications. You may also feel happiest if you can avoid signing important agreements or contracts during these times.

To plot the progress of Mercury, fill in the blank diagram on page 8, writing '1' in the section next to your Sun sign, then numbering consecutively in an anti-clockwise direction around the signs until you have completed them all. It will now be easy to chart Mercury's movements. When it is in the same sign as your Sun, Mercury is in your first house, when he moves into the next sign (assuming he's not going retrograde) he occupies your second house, and so on, until he reaches your twelfth house, at which point he will move back into your first house again.

Diagram 1

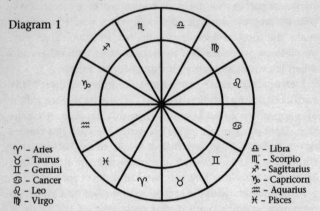

♈︎ – Aries
♉︎ – Taurus
♊︎ – Gemini
♋︎ – Cancer
♌︎ – Leo
♍︎ – Virgo

♎︎ – Libra
♏︎ – Scorpio
♐︎ – Sagittarius
♑︎ – Capricorn
♒︎ – Aquarius
♓︎ – Pisces

Here are the houses of the horoscope, numbered from one to twelve, for someone born with the Sun in Aquarius.

Diagram 2

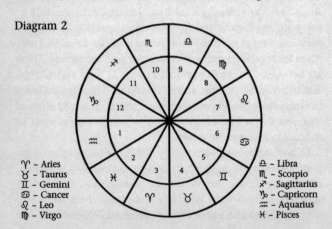

♈︎ – Aries
♉︎ – Taurus
♊︎ – Gemini
♋︎ – Cancer
♌︎ – Leo
♍︎ – Virgo

♎︎ – Libra
♏︎ – Scorpio
♐︎ – Sagittarius
♑︎ – Capricorn
♒︎ – Aquarius
♓︎ – Pisces

MERCURY'S ENTRY INTO THE SIGNS IN 2000
(All times are given in GMT, using the 24-hour clock)

January
Mercury is in Capricorn when 2000 begins

18	22:21	Aquarius

February

5	08:10	Pisces
21	12:47	Retrograde in Pisces

March

14	20:40	Direct in Pisces

April

13	00:18	Aries
30	03:54	Taurus

May

14	07:11	Gemini
30	04:28	Cancer

June

23	08:33	Retrograde in Cancer

July

17	13:21	Direct in Cancer

August

7	05:43	Leo
22	10:12	Virgo

September

7	21:23	Libra
28	13:29	Scorpio

October

18	13:42	Retrograde in Scorpio

November
7	07:29	Retrograde into Libra
8	02:29	Direct in Libra
8	21:43	Scorpio

December
3	20:27	Sagittarius
23	02:04	Capricorn

As 2000 begins, Mercury is moving through the final degrees of Capricorn, so it is in whichever house corresponds with the sign of Capricorn in your diagram. For instance, if you're an Aquarian, Mercury will move into your own sign at 22:21 GMT on 18 January and will occupy your first house. You can then read the explanation below telling you what to expect at this time. Mercury next moves signs at 08:10 GMT on 5 February, when he moves into Pisces. So if you're an Aquarian, Mercury will now be in your second house.

Mercury in the First House

This is a very busy time for you and you're completely wrapped up in your own ideas and concerns. Even if you aren't usually very chatty, you certainly are at the moment. However, you will much prefer talking about yourself to listening to other people! You've got lots of nervous energy at the moment and you'll enjoy getting out and about as much as possible. Look for ways of burning off excess energy, such as going for brisk walks or doing things that require initiative. This is a great opportunity to think about ways of pushing forward with ideas and getting new projects off the ground.

Mercury in the Second House

This is a great time to think about things that mean a lot to you. These might be beliefs, philosophies or anything else that gives meaning to your life. It's also a good time to consider the people that make your world go round. Do you devote enough time to them? You should also spare a thought for your finances, because this is a perfect opportunity to scrutinize them and make sure everything is in order. You could get in touch with someone who can give you some financial advice, or you might do some research into how to put your money to good use.

Mercury in the Third House

Chatty? You bet! This is probably when you're at your most talkative, and you'll enjoy nattering away about whatever pops into your head. You'll love talking to whoever happens to be around, but you'll get on especially well with neighbours, people you see in the course of your daily routine and close relatives. You'll soon start to feel restless if you have to spend too long in one place, so grab every opportunity to vary your schedule. You'll love taking off on day trips, going away for weekend breaks or simply abandoning your usual routine and doing something completely different. Communications will go well and you'll love playing with gadgets and appliances.

Mercury in the Fourth House

Your thoughts are never far away from your home and family life at the moment. You may be thinking about ways of improving your living standards and you could talk to people who can give you some advice. You're also wrapped up in thoughts of the past, and you may even be assailed by memories of far-off events or things you haven't thought about in ages. Pay attention to your dreams because they could give you some invaluable insights into the way you're feeling. Watch out for a slight tendency to be defensive or to imagine that people are trying to get at you. It's a lovely time for getting in touch with your nearest and dearest who live a long way away.

Mercury in the Fifth House

You'll really enjoy putting your mind to good use at the moment, especially if you do things that are based on fun. For instance, you might get engrossed in competitions, jigsaw puzzles, crosswords and quizzes, especially if there's the chance of winning a prize! Children and pets will be terrific company and you'll love romping with them. However, you may find that they're a lot more playful than usual. You may even be on the receiving end of some practical jokes. It's a super time to go on holiday, particularly if you're visiting somewhere you've never been before. Your social life promises to keep you busy and you'll find it easy to talk to loved ones about things that matter to you.

Mercury in the Sixth House

This is the ideal time of year to think about your health and well-being. Are you looking after yourself properly? If you've been battling with some strange symptoms, this is the perfect opportunity to get them investigated so you can put your mind at rest. You'll enjoy reading about medical matters, such as immersing yourself in a book that tells you how to keep fit or extolling the virtues of a specific eating plan. Your work might also keep you busy. Colleagues and customers will be chatty, and you could spend a lot of time dealing with paperwork or tapping away on the computer. It's a great time to look for a new job, especially if that means scanning the newspaper adverts, joining an employment agency or writing lots of application letters.

Mercury in the Seventh House

Communications play an important role in all your relationships at the moment. This is your chance to put across your point of view and to keep other people posted about what you think. You may enjoy having lots of chats with partners or you might have something important to discuss. Either way, the key to success is to keep talking! You're prepared to reach a compromise, so it's a marvellous time to get involved in negotiations and discussions. You'll also find that two heads are better than one right now, so it's the ideal time to do some teamwork. You'll enjoy bouncing your ideas off other people and listening to what they have to say.

Mercury in the Eighth House

It's time to turn your attention to your shared resources and official money matters. So if you share a bank account with your partner, you should check that everything is running smoothly. You might even decide to open a new account that suits you better or that pays a higher rate of interest. Speaking of accounts, this is an excellent time to fill in your tax return or complete your accounts for the year because you're in the right frame of mind for such things. This is also a good time to think about your close relationships. Do they bring you the emotional satisfaction that you need or is something missing? If you think there's room for improvement, talk to your partner about how to make things better between you.

Mercury in the Ninth House

The more you can expand your mental and physical horizons now, the happier you'll be. It's a time of year when you're filled with intellectual curiosity about the world and you long to cram your head with all sorts of facts and figures. You might decide to do some studying, whether you do it on a very informal basis or enrol for an evening class or college course. You'll certainly enjoy browsing around bookshops and library shelves, looking for books on your favourite subjects. Travel will appeal to you too, especially if you can visit somewhere exotic or a place that you've never been to before. You might become interested in a different religion from your own or you could be engrossed in something connected with philosophy, history or spirituality.

Mercury in the Tenth House

Spend some time thinking about your career prospects. Are you happy with the way things are going or does your professional life need a rethink? This is a great opportunity to talk to people who can give you some good advice. It's also an excellent time to share your ideas with your boss or a superior, especially if you're hoping to impress them. You could hear about a promotion or some improved job prospects, or you might decide to apply for a completely new job. It's also a marvellous opportunity to increase your qualifications, perhaps by training for something new or brushing up on an existing skill. You'll find it easier than usual to talk to older friends and relatives, especially if they can sometimes be a little tricky or hard to please.

Mercury in the Eleventh House

This is a great time to enjoy the company of friends and acquaintances. You'll love talking to them, especially if you can chat about subjects that make you think or that have humanitarian overtones. All sorts of intellectual activities will appeal to you at the moment. If your social circle is getting smaller and smaller, grab this chance to widen your horizons by meeting people who are on the same wavelength as you. For instance, you might decide to join a new club or society that caters for one of your interests. It's also a good opportunity to think about your hopes and wishes for the future. Are they going according to plan, or should you revise your strategy or even start again from scratch?

Mercury in the Twelfth House

You're entering a very reflective and reclusive period when you want to retreat from the madding crowd and have some time to yourself. You might enjoy taking the phone off the hook and curling up with a good book, or you could spend time studying subjects by yourself. There will be times when you feel quite tongue-tied, and you'll find it difficult to say exactly what you mean. You may even want to maintain a discreet silence on certain subjects, but make sure that other people don't take advantage of this by putting words into your mouth. You could be the recipient of someone's confidences, in which case you'll be a sympathetic listener. If you want to tell someone your secrets, choose your confidante wisely.

LOVE AND THE STARS

Love makes the world go round. When we know we're loved, we walk on air. We feel confident, happy and joyous. Without love, we feel miserable, lonely and as if life isn't worth living. If you're still looking for your perfect partner, this is the ideal guide for you. It will tell you which Sun signs you get on best with and which ones aren't such easy-going mates. By the way, there is hope for every astrological combination, and none are out and out disasters. It's simply that you'll find it easier to get on well with some signs than with others.

At the end of this section you'll see two compatibility charts – one showing how you get on in the love and sex stakes, and the other one telling you which signs make the best friends. These charts will instantly remind you which signs get on best and which struggle to keep the peace. Each combination has been given marks out of ten, with ten points being a fabulous pairing and one point being pretty grim. Find the woman's Sun sign along the top line of the chart, then look down the left-hand column for the man's sign. The square where these two lines meet will give you the result of this astrological combination. For instance, when assessing the love and sex compatibility of a Leo woman and a Cancerian man, they score six out of ten.

♎ Libra

Of all the members of the zodiac, this is the one that finds it easiest to get on with the other signs. Librans get on particularly well with Geminis and Aquarians, their fellow Air signs. A Libran is enchanted by a Gemini's quick brain and ready wit, and they enjoy endless discussions on all sorts of subjects. When two Librans get together, they revel in the resulting harmonious atmosphere but it's almost impossible for them to reach any decisions – each one defers to the other while being unable to say what they really want. A Libran is intrigued by the independence and sharp mind of an Aquarian, but their feelings could be hurt by the Aquarian's emotional coolness.

Libra enjoys being with the three Fire signs – Aries, Leo and Sagittarius. Libra, who often takes life at rather a slow pace, is energized by a lively Arien, and they complement one another's personalities well. However, the Libran may occasionally feel hurt by the Arien's single-mindedness and blunt speech. A Libran adores the luxury-loving ways of a Leo, and they'll both spend a fortune in the pursuit of happiness. They also get on well in the bedroom. When a Libran gets together with an exuberant Sagittarian, they'll have great fun. All the same, the Sagittarian need for honesty could fluster the Libran, who adopts a much more diplomatic approach to life.

Although the other two Air signs can find it hard to understand members of the Water element, it's different for Librans. They're more sympathetic to the emotional energies of Cancerians, Scorpios and Pisceans. A Libran delights in the protective care of a Cancerian, but those ever-changing Cancerians moods may be hard for a balanced Libran to take. Those deep Scorpio emotions will intrigue the Libran but they may quickly become bogged down by such an intense outlook on life and will be desperate for some light relief. As for Pisces, the Libran is charmed by the Piscean's delicate nature and creative gifts, but both signs hate facing up to unpleasant facts so this couple may never deal with any problems that lie between them.

Libra enjoys the reliable natures of Taurus, Virgo and Capricorn, the Earth signs. A Libran appreciates the company of a relaxed and easy-going Taurean, although they may sometimes regret the Taurean's lack of imagination. When a Libran and a Virgo get together, the Libran enjoys the Virgo's mental abilities but their critical comments will soon cut the Libran to the quick. The Libran may not come back for a second tongue-lashing. A Libran understands the ambitions of a Capricorn, and likes their steady nature and the way they support their family. However, there could soon be rows about money, with the Libran spending a lot more than the Capricorn thinks is necessary.

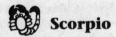 **Scorpio**

Not every sign gets on well with its fellow members, yet an astonishing number of Scorpios pair up. They feel safe together because they know the worst and best about each other. When things are good, they're brilliant but these two can also bring out the worst in each other, with intense silences and brooding sulks. A Scorpio enjoys the tender ministrations of a loving Cancerian, and adores being with someone who's so obviously concerned about their welfare. Feelings run deep when a Scorpio pairs up with a Piscean, although the Scorpio may become impatient with the Piscean's reluctance to face up to unpalatable truths.

The three Earth signs, Taurus, Virgo and Capricorn, are well-suited to the Scorpio temperament. Those astrological opposites, Scorpio and Taurus, enjoy a powerful relationship, much of which probably takes place in the bedroom, but whenever they have a disagreement there's an atmosphere you could cut with a knife, and neither of them will be prepared to admit they were in the wrong. A Scorpio is attracted to a neat, analytical Virgo but their feelings will be hurt by this sign's tendency to criticize. What's more, their pride stops them telling the Virgo how they feel. The Scorpio admires a practical Capricorn, especially if they've earned a lot of respect through their work, but this could be a rather chilly pairing because both signs find it difficult to show their feelings.

When you put a Scorpio together with one of the three Fire signs, they'll either get on famously or won't understand one another at all. A Scorpio revels in the lusty Arien's sex drive, although they'll soon feel tired if they try to keep up with the Arien's busy schedule. The combination of Scorpio and Leo packs quite a punch. They're both very strong personalities, but they boss one another around like mad and find it almost impossible to achieve a compromise if they fall out. A Scorpio likes to take life at a measured pace, so they're bemused by a Sagittarian's need to keep busy all the time. In the end, they'll become fed up with never seeing the Sagittarian, or playing second fiddle to all their other interests.

Scorpio is bemused by the three Air signs – Gemini, Libran and Aquarius – because they operate on such completely different wavelengths. A Scorpio can be good friends with a Gemini but they're at emotional cross-purposes, with the Scorpio's intense approach to life too much for a light-hearted Gemini to cope with. Emotions are also the bugbear between a Scorpio and a Libran. Everything is great at first, but the Scorpio's powerful feelings and dark moods will eventually send the Libran running in the opposite direction. You can expect some tense arguments when a Scorpio pairs up with an Aquarian – they're both convinced that they're right and the other one is wrong.

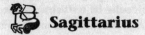 Sagittarius

When a Sagittarian pairs up with a fellow Fire sign, there's plenty of warmth and the odd firework. A Sagittarian is thrilled by the adventurous spirit of an Arien, and they love exploring the world together. There are plenty of tall tales when a Sagittarian gets together with a Leo – they'll try to outdo each other, dropping names and recounting their greatest triumphs. If the Leo is slightly pompous, the Sagittarian is able to take them down a peg or two, but they must beware of hurting the Leo's feelings. As for two Sagittarians, they'll spur each other on and encourage one another to gain as much experience of life as possible. You probably won't be able to move in their house for books.

With their endless curiosity about the world, Sagittarians understand the intellectual Air signs very well. A Sagittarian enjoys the chatty company of a Gemini and, because they're opposite numbers in the zodiac, the Sagittarian is able to encourage the Gemini to see things through and explore them in more detail than usual. A refined and diplomatic Libran will try to teach the blunt Sagittarian not to say the first thing that pops into their head. However, the Sagittarian may eventually find the Libran's sense of balance rather trying – why can't they get more worked up about things? There's plenty of straight talking when a Sagittarian teams up with an Aquarian – they both have a high regard for honesty. The independent Sagittarian respects the Aquarian's need for freedom, but may feel rather stung by their periods of emotional coolness.

A Sagittarian will struggle to understand the Earth signs. They respect the Taurean's ability to work hard but they're driven to distraction by their reluctance to make changes and break out of any ruts they've fallen into. A Sagittarian enjoys talking to a brainy Virgo, but their expansive and spontaneous nature could eventually be restricted by the Virgo's need to think things through before taking action. When a Sagittarian gets together with a Capricorn, it's a case of optimism versus pessimism. While the Sagittarian's glass is half-full, the Capricorn's is always half-empty, and this causes many rows and possibly some ill feeling.

There could be lots of misunderstandings when a Sagittarian gets involved with one of the Water signs. A Sagittarian needs a bigger social circle than their family, whereas a Cancerian is quite happy surrounded by kith and kin. The Sagittarian need for independence won't go down well, either. It's like oil and water when a Sagittarian pairs up with a Scorpio. The Sagittarian is the roamer of the zodiac, whereas the Scorpio wants them where they can see them, in case they're up to no good. All will be well if the Sagittarian gets together with a strong-minded Piscean. In fact, they'll really enjoy one another's company. A Piscean who's lost in a world of their own, however, will soon leave them cold.

 **Capricorn**

Despite their outward poise, a Capricorn is very easily hurt so they need to know their feelings won't be trampled on. There's least danger of that when they get together with a fellow Earth sign. A Capricorn adores a Taurean's deep sense of responsibility and they'll both work hard to create their ideal home. A Capricorn appreciates the methodical approach of a Virgo, but could feel deeply hurt by the Virgo's sharp tongue and caustic remarks. If two Capricorns team up, one of them must be demonstrative and openly affectionate otherwise the relationship could be rather sterile and serious.

Capricorns also feel safe with members of the Water signs. When a Capricorn gets together with a Cancerian, they do their utmost to make their home a haven. They'll get great satisfaction from channelling their energies into bringing up a family. A Capricorn may be rather bemused by the depth and intensity of a Scorpio's emotions – Capricorns are too reserved to indulge in such drama themselves and it can make them feel uncomfortable. A no-nonsense Capricorn could be perplexed by an extremely vulnerable Piscean and won't know how to handle them. Should they give them a hanky or tell them to pull themselves together?

The Air signs can also make a Capricorn feel somewhat unsettled. They're fascinated by a Gemini's breadth of knowledge and endless chat, but they also find them superficial and rather flighty. In fact, the Capricorn probably doesn't trust the Gemini. A Capricorn feels far happier in the company of a Libran. Here's someone who seems much steadier emotionally and who can help the Capricorn to unwind after a hard day's work. It can be great or ghastly when a Capricorn sets their sights on an Aquarian. They understand each other provided the Aquarian isn't too unconventional, but the Capricorn feels uncomfortable and embarrassed by any displays of eccentricity, deliberate or not.

The Fire signs help to warm up the Capricorn, who can be rather remote and distant at times. A Capricorn admires the Arien's drive and initiative, but endlessly tells them to look before they leap and could become irritated when they don't take this sage advice. When a Capricorn gets together with a Leo, they won't need to worry about appearances – the Capricorn will feel justly proud of the smart Leo. However, they could wince when the bills come in and they discover how much those clothes cost. A Capricorn thinks a Sagittarian must have come from another planet – how can they be so relaxed and laid-back all the time? They have great respect for the Sagittarian's wisdom and philosophy, but they quickly become fed up with having to fit in around the Sagittarian's hectic social life.

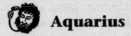 **Aquarius**

Put an Aquarian with a fellow Air sign and they're happy. They thoroughly enjoy being with a lively Gemini and love discussing everything under the sun with them. They may not have a very exciting sex life, but their mental closeness will more than make up for it. The gentle charms of a Libran calms down an Aquarian when their nerves become frayed, although they disapprove of the Libran's innate tact and diplomacy – why can't they just say what they think, instead of sitting on the fence? With two Aquarians you never know what to expect, other than that they'll be great friends. They'll certainly do a lot of talking, but could spend more time debating esoteric ideas and abstract concepts.

An Aquarian likes all the Fire signs, although they find Ariens hard to fathom and can become exhausted by an Arien's endless supply of energy and enthusiasm. There are no such problems when an Aquarian pairs up with a Leo because they complement each other in many ways. The Aquarian teaches objectivity to the Leo, who in return encourages the Aquarian to express their emotions more. An Aquarian thoroughly enjoys being with a Sagittarian because both of them hate being tied down. As a result, they respect one another's independence and will probably rarely see each other because of all their spare-time activities.

It's not quite so simple when an Aquarian joins forces with one of the Earth signs. An Aquarian will lock horns with a Taurean sooner or later, because neither of them is able to back down once a disagreement has started. The Aquarian will also feel very restricted by the Taurean's possessiveness. The Virgo's analytical approach to life intrigues the Aquarian but they'll sit up all night arguing the toss over everything, with each one convinced that they've got all the answers. When an Aquarian meets a Capricorn, they've got their work cut out for them if they're to find a happy medium between the erratic Aquarian and the conventional Capricorn.

An Aquarian feels out of their depth when they're with one of the Water signs. They simply don't understand what makes a Cancerian tick – why do they worry themselves sick over things that they can't change? The Aquarian finds it all most peculiar. They also find it difficult to understand a Scorpio who takes so many things so seriously. Although the Aquarian also has a list of topics that mean a lot to them, they're not the sort of things that hold the slightest interest for a Scorpio. It's more or less the same story with a Pisces, because their huge resources of emotion make the Aquarian feel uncomfortable and fill them with a strong desire to escape as fast as possible.

 **Pisces**

Relationships mean a lot to a sensitive Piscean, but they're easily misunderstood by many of the more robust signs. There are no such worries with the other Water signs, however. A Piscean loves being with a tender Cancerian who knows how to help them relax and feel safe. They really enjoy playing house together but the emotional scenes will blow the roof off. The relationship between a Piscean and a Scorpio can be quite spicy and sexy, but the Piscean is turned off if the Scorpio becomes too intense and dramatic. Two Pisceans feel safe with one another, but they'll push all their problems under the carpet unless one of them is more objective.

A Piscean also gets on well with the Earth signs, although with a few reservations. A Piscean takes comfort from being looked after by a protective Taurean, but after a while they could feel stifled by the Taurean's possessive and matter-of-fact attitude. The relationship between a Piscean and a Virgo starts off well but the Piscean could soon feel crushed by the Virgo's criticism and will need more emotional reassurance than the Virgo is able to give. A Piscean feels safe with a Capricorn because they're so dependable but in the end this may begin to bug them. It's not that they want the Capricorn to two-time them, more that they'd like a little unpredictability every now and then.

A Piscean is fascinated by the Air signs but their apparent lack of emotion could cause problems. A Piscean and a Gemini are terrific friends but could encounter difficulties as lovers. The Piscean's strong emotional needs are too much for the Gemini to handle – they'll feel as if they're drowning. The Piscean is on much firmer ground with a Libran, who'll go out of their way to keep the Piscean happy. Neither sign is good at facing up to any nasty truths, however. An Aquarian is too much for a sensitive Piscean, who views the world through rose-coloured specs. An Aquarian, on the other hand, has uncomfortably clear vision.

The Fire signs can cheer up a Piscean enormously, but any prolonged displays of emotion will make the Fire signs feel weighed down. The Piscean is fascinated by an Arien's exploits but could feel reluctant to join in. They'll also be easily hurt by some of the Arien's off-the-cuff remarks. When a Piscean pairs up with a Leo they appreciate the way the Leo wants to take charge and look after them. After a while, however, this could grate on them and they'll want to be more independent. A Piscean enjoys discussing philosophy and spiritual ideas with a Sagittarian – they can sit up half the night talking things through. The Sagittarian brand of honesty could hurt the Piscean at times, but they know this isn't malicious and will quickly forgive such outbursts.

 Aries

Because Ariens belong to the Fire element, they get on very well with their fellow Fire signs Leo and Sagittarius. All the same, an Arien getting together with a Leo will soon notice a distinct drop in their bank balance, because they'll enjoy going to all the swankiest restaurants and sitting in the best seats at the theatre. When an Arien pairs up with a Sagittarian, they'll compete over who drives the fastest car and has the most exciting holidays. When two Ariens get together the results can be combustible. Ideally, one Arien should be a lot quieter, otherwise they'll spend most of their time jostling for power. All these combinations are very sexy and physical.

Ariens also thrive in the company of the three Air signs – Gemini, Libra and Aquarius. Of the three, they get on best with Geminis, who share their rather childlike view of the world and also their sense of fun. An Arien and a Gemini enjoy hatching all sorts of ideas and schemes, even if they never get round to putting them into action. There's an exciting sense of friction between Aries and Libra, their opposite number in the zodiac. An Arien will be enchanted by the way their Libran caters to their every need, but may become impatient when the Libran also wants to look after other people. An Arien will be captivated by the originality of an Aquarian, although at times they'll be driven mad by the Aquarian's eccentric approach to life and the way they blow hot and cold in the bedroom.

Ariens don't do so well with the Earth signs – Taurus, Virgo and Capricorn. The very careful, slightly plodding nature of a typical Taurean can drive an Arien barmy at times, and although they'll respect – and benefit from – the Taurean's practical approach to life, it can still fill them with irritation. An Arien finds it difficult to fathom a Virgo, because their attitudes to life are diametrically opposed. An Arien likes to jump in with both feet, while a Virgo prefers to take things slowly and analyse every possibility before committing themselves. An Arien can get on quite well with a Capricorn, because they're linked by their sense of ambition and their earthy sexual needs.

An Arien is out of their depth with any of the Water signs – Cancer, Scorpio and Pisces. They quickly become irritated by the defensive Cancerian, although they'll love their cooking. An Arien will enjoy a very passionate affair with a Scorpio, but the Scorpio's need to know exactly what the Arien is up to when their back is turned will soon cause problems and rifts. Although an Arien may begin a relationship with a Pisces by wanting to look after them and protect them from the harsh realities of life, eventually the Piscean's extremely sensitive nature may bring out the Arien's bullying streak.

 **Taurus**

Taureans are literally in their element when they're with Virgos or Capricorns who, like themselves, are Earth signs. Two Taureans will get along very happily together, although they could become so wedded to routine that they get stuck in a rut. They may also encourage one another to eat too much. A Taurean will enjoy being with a Virgo, because they respect the Virgo's methodical nature. They'll also like encouraging their Virgo to relax and take life easy. Money will form a link between a Taurean and a Capricorn, with plenty of serious discussions on how to make it and what to do with it once they've got it. There will also be a strong sexual rapport, and the Taurean will encourage the more sensual side of the Capricorn.

The relationship between a Taurean and members of the Water element is also very good. A Taurean and a Cancerian will revel in one another's company and will probably be so happy at home that they'll rarely stir from their armchairs. They both have a strong need for emotional security and will stick together through thick and thin. There's plenty of passion when a Taurean pairs up with a Scorpio, although the faithful Taurean could become fed up with the Scorpio's jealous nature. They simply won't understand what they're being accused of, and their loyal nature will be offended by the very thought that they could be a two-timer. A Taurean will be delighted by a delicate Piscean, and will want to take care of such a vulnerable and sensitive creature.

Things become rather more complicated when a Taurean pairs up with an Arien, Leo or Sagittarian, all of whom are Fire signs. They have very little in common – Taureans like to take things slowly while Fire signs want to make things happen *now*. It's particularly difficult between a Taurean and an Arien – the careful Taurean will feel harried and rushed by the impetuous Arien. It's a little better when a Taurean gets together with a Leo, because they share a deep appreciation of the good things in life, although the Taurean will be horrified by the Leo's ability to spend money. Making joint decisions could be difficult, however, because they'll both stand their ground and refuse to budge. A Taurean and a Sagittarian simply don't understand each other – they're on such different wavelengths. Any Taurean displays of possessiveness will make the independent Sagittarian want to run a mile.

Taureans are equally mystified by the Air signs – Gemini, Libra and Aquarius. What they see as the flightiness of Gemini drives them barmy – why can't the Gemini settle down and do one thing at a time? The Taurean will probably feel quite exhausted by the Gemini's many interests and bubbly character. Taurus and Libra are a surprisingly good pairing, because they share a need for beauty, luxury and love. This could end up costing the penny-wise Taurean quite a packet, but they'll have a deliciously romantic time along the way. Taurus and Aquarius are chalk and cheese, and neither one is prepared to meet the other one halfway. The Taurean need to keep tabs on their loved one's every movement will irritate the freedom-loving Aquarian, and there will be plenty of rows as a result.

🏃🏃 Gemini

One of the Air signs, Geminis get on very well with their fellow members of this element – Librans and Aquarians. Two Geminis are the astrological equivalent of double trouble – they chat nineteen to the dozen and revel in the company of someone who understands them so well. A Gemini delights in being with a Libran, because they enjoy the intellectual company and will benefit from the Libran's (usually) relaxed approach to life. They'll also learn to deal with their emotions more if a sympathetic Libran can guide them. Gemini and Aquarius is a very exciting pairing – the Gemini is encouraged to think deeply and knows that the Aquarian won't put up with any woolly ideas or fudged arguments.

Geminis also get on well with the three Fire signs – Aries, Leo and Sagittarius. A Gemini loves being with a racy, adventurous Arien, and together they enjoy keeping abreast of all the latest gossip and cultural developments. However, after the first flush of enthusiasm has worn off, the Gemini may find the Arien's strong need for sex rather hard to take. The Gemini gets on very well with a Leo. They delight in the Leo's affectionate nature and are amused by their need to have the best that money can buy – and they'll gladly share in the spoils. Gemini and Sagittarius are an excellent combination, because they sit opposite each other in the zodiac and so complement one another's character. The Gemini will be fascinated by the erudite and knowledgeable Sagittarian.

Gemini doesn't do so well with the Earth signs of Taurus and Capricorn, although they get on better with Virgo. The Gemini finds it difficult to understand a Taurean, because they see the world from such different viewpoints. The Gemini takes a more light-hearted approach and lives life at such a speed that they find it difficult to slow down to the more measured pace of a Taurean. The wonderfully dry Capricorn sense of humour is a source of constant delight to a Gemini. However, they're less taken with the Capricorn's streak of pessimism and their love of tradition. Of the three Earth signs, Gemini and Virgo are the most compatible. The Gemini shares the Virgo's brainpower and they have long, fascinating conversations.

When a Gemini gets together with the Water signs, the result can be enjoyable or puzzling. Gemini and Cancer have little in common, because the Gemini wants to spread their emotional and intellectual wings, whereas a Cancerian likes to stay close to home and has little interest in abstract ideas. Gemini finds Scorpio perplexing because they operate on such different levels. A Gemini tends to skim along the surface of things, so often deals with life on a superficial level, whereas a Scorpio likes to dig deep and has to have an emotional investment in everything they do. A Gemini appreciates the subtlety and sensitivity of a Piscean, but they're likely to make off-the-cuff comments that unwittingly hurt the Piscean.

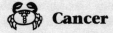 **Cancer**

Cancerians revel in the company of their fellow Water signs of Scorpio and Pisces. When two Cancerians get together they could spend most of their time at home or eating – preferably both. They feel safe in the knowledge that they both have a strong need for love, but their innate Cancerian tenacity may mean they cling on to the relationship even if it's long past its best. A Cancerian is enchanted with a Scorpio, because at last they feel free to really let rip emotionally. However, the intuitive Cancerian should beware of soaking up the Scorpio's darker moods like a psychic sponge. A Cancerian will take one look at a delicate Piscean and want to invite them home for a good hot meal. All the Cancerian's protective instincts are aroused by a gentle Piscean, but their anger will also be aroused if it turns out the Piscean has been leading a double life behind their back.

Cancerians also find a great deal of comfort in the company of the Earth signs – Taurus, Virgo and Capricorn. Cancer and Taurus were made for each other – they both adore home comforts and they trust one another implicitly. The Cancerian loves making a cosy nest for their hard-working Taurean. A Cancerian finds a Virgo a more difficult proposition, especially emotionally. Whereas Cancer is all warm hugs and holding hands by the fire, Virgo prefers to read a book and reserve any displays of affection for the bedroom. Cancer and Capricorn are opposite numbers in the zodiac, so share a tremendous rapport. They also share the same values of home, tradition and family, and if anyone can help a Capricorn to relax and take life easy, it's a Cancerian.

Life becomes more difficult when it comes to a Cancerian's relationship with any of the Air signs. They simply don't understand one another. A Cancerian can't make a Gemini out. They feel confused by what they think of as the Gemini's flightiness and inability to stay in one place for long. They can also be easily hurt by the Gemini's difficulty in expressing their emotions. A Cancerian gets on much better with a Libran. They're both ambitious in their own ways and so have a great deal in common. The Cancerian enjoys the Libran's romantic nature, but the Cancerian tendency to cling doesn't go down well. A Cancerian regards a typical Aquarian as a being from another planet. They're hurt by the Aquarian's strong need for independence and dislike of having to account for their every action, and are dismayed and confused by the Aquarian's hot-and-cold attitude to sex.

The Fire signs of Aries, Leo and Sagittarius are also a potential source of bewilderment to the gentle Cancerian. They understand the drive and ambition of an Arien, but will be stung by their blunt speech and worried about their daredevil tendencies. What if they hurt themselves? A Cancerian gets on well with a Leo because they share a strong love of family and are both openly affectionate and loving. The Cancerian enjoys creating a home that the Leo can feel proud of. So far, so good, but the story isn't so simple when a Cancerian pairs up with a Sagittarian. They're too different to understand one another – the Cancerian wants to stay at home with the family while the Sagittarian has an instinctive need to roam the world. As a result, the Cancerian will be disappointed, and then hurt, when the Sagittarian's busy schedule takes them away from home too often.

 Leo

Leos adore the company of their fellow Fire signs, Ariens and Sagittarius. They understand one another and enjoy each other's spontaneous warmth and affection. A Leo is amused by the exuberance and impulsiveness of an Arien, and they enjoy being persuaded to let their hair down a bit and not worry too much about appearances. A Leo enjoys the dash and vitality of a Sagittarian, although they may feel irritated if they can never get hold of them on the phone or the Sagittarian is always off doing other things. Two Leos together either love or loathe one another. One of them should be prepared to take a back seat otherwise they'll both be vying for the limelight all the time.

The three Air signs of Gemini, Libra and Aquarius all get on well with Leos. When a Leo pairs up with a Gemini, you can expect lots of laughter and plenty of fascinating conversations. The demonstrative Leo is able to help the Gemini be more openly affectionate and loving. Leo and Libra is a great combination, and the Leo is enchanted by the Libran's fair-minded attitude. Both signs love luxury and all the good things in life but their bank managers may not be so pleased by the amount of the money they manage to spend. Leo and Aquarius sit opposite one another across the horoscope, so they already have a great deal in common. They're fascinated by one another but they're both very stubborn, so any disputes between them usually end in stalemate because neither is prepared to concede any ground.

Leos don't really understand the Earth signs. Although Leos admire their practical approach to life, they find it rather restricting. A Leo enjoys the sensuous and hedonistic side of a Taurean's character but may become frustrated by their fear of change. Leo and Virgo have very little in common, especially when it comes to food – the Leo wants to tuck in at all the best restaurants while the Virgo is worried about the state of the kitchens, the number of calories and the size of the bill. A Leo respects the Capricorn's desire to support their family and approves of their need to be seen in the best possible light, but they feel hurt by the Capricorn's difficulty in showing their feelings.

When a Leo gets together with one of the Water signs – Cancer, Scorpio or Pisces – they'll enjoy the sexual side of the relationship but could eventually feel stifled by all that Watery emotion. A Leo and a Cancerian adore making a home together and both dote on their children. The Leo also likes comforting their vulnerable Cancerian – provided this doesn't happen too often. A Leo and a Scorpio will be powerfully attracted to one another, but power could also pull them apart – who's going to wear the trousers? They'll also lock horns during rows and both of them will refuse to back down. A Leo delights in a sophisticated Piscean, but may become irritated by their indecision and jangly nerves.

 **Virgo**

As you might imagine, Virgos are happy with their fellow Earth signs of Taurus and Capricorn because they share the same practical attitude. A Virgo enjoys the steady, reassuring company of a Taurean, and they might even learn to relax a little instead of worrying themselves into the ground over the slightest problem. When two Virgos get together it can be too much of a good thing. Although at first they'll love talking to someone who shares so many of their preoccupations and ideas, they can soon drive one another round the bend. When a Virgo first meets a Capricorn they're delighted to know someone who's obviously got their head screwed on. It's only later on that they wish the Capricorn could lighten up every now and then.

Virgos get on well with Cancerians, Scorpios and Pisceans, the three Water signs. A Virgo enjoys being looked after by a considerate Cancerian, although they'll worry about their waistline and may get irritated by the Cancerian's super-sensitive feelings. You can expect plenty of long, analytical conversations when a Virgo gets together with a Scorpio. They both love getting to the bottom of subjects and will endlessly talk things through. They'll also get on extremely well in the bedroom. Pisces is Virgo's opposite sign, but although some opposites thrive in each other's company, that isn't always the case with this combination. The Virgo could soon grow impatient with the dreamy Piscean and will long to tell them a few home truths.

Although the other Earth signs don't usually get on well with Air signs, it's different for Virgos. They understand the intellectual energies of Geminis, Librans and Aquarians. A Virgo thrives in a Gemini's company, and they spend hours chatting over the phone if they can't get together in person. It's difficult for them to discuss their emotions, however, and they may never tell each other how they really feel. A Virgo admires a sophisticated, charming Libran, and marvels at their diplomacy. How do they do it? Expect a few sparks to fly when a Virgo pairs up with an Aquarian, because both of them have very strong opinions and aren't afraid to air them. The result is a lot of hot air and some vigorous arguments.

The three Fire signs – Aries, Leo and Sagittarius – are a source of endless fascination to a Virgo. They've got so much energy! A Virgo finds an Arien exciting but their relationship could be short-lived because the Virgo will be so irritated by the Arien's devil-may-care attitude to life. When a Virgo pairs up with a Leo, they'll be intrigued by this person's comparatively lavish lifestyle but their own modest temperament will be shocked if the Leo enjoys showing off. A Virgo is able to talk to a Sagittarius until the cows come home – they're both fascinated by ideas, although the precise Virgo will first be amused, and then irritated, by the Sagittarian's rather relaxed attitude to hard facts.

Compatibility in Love and Sex at a glance

M\F	♈	♉	♊	♋	♌	♍	♎	♏	♐	♑	♒	♓
♈	8	5	9	7	9	4	7	8	9	7	7	3
♉	6	8	4	10	7	8	8	7	3	8	2	8
♊	8	2	7	3	8	7	9	4	9	4	9	4
♋	5	10	4	8	6	5	6	8	2	9	2	8
♌	9	8	9	7	7	4	9	6	8	7	9	6
♍	4	8	6	4	4	7	6	7	7	9	4	4
♎	7	8	10	7	8	5	9	6	9	6	10	6
♏	7	9	4	7	6	6	7	10	5	6	5	7
♐	9	4	10	4	9	7	8	4	9	6	9	5
♑	7	8	4	9	6	8	6	4	4	8	4	5
♒	8	6	9	4	9	4	9	6	8	7	8	2
♓	7	6	7	9	6	7	6	9	7	5	4	9

1 = the pits
10 = the peaks

Key

♈ – Aries
♉ – Taurus
♊ – Gemini
♋ – Cancer
♌ – Leo
♍ – Virgo

♎ – Libra
♏ – Scorpio
♐ – Sagittarius
♑ – Capricorn
♒ – Aquarius
♓ – Pisces

Compatibility in Friendship at a glance

F / M	♈	♉	♊	♋	♌	♍	♎	♏	♐	♑	♒	♓
♈	8	5	10	5	9	3	7	8	9	6	8	5
♉	6	9	6	10	7	8	7	6	4	9	3	9
♊	9	3	9	4	9	8	10	5	10	5	10	6
♋	6	9	4	9	5	4	6	9	4	10	3	9
♌	10	7	9	6	9	4	8	6	9	6	9	7
♍	5	9	8	4	4	8	5	8	8	10	5	6
♎	8	9	10	8	8	6	9	5	9	6	10	7
♏	7	8	5	8	7	7	6	9	4	5	6	8
♐	9	5	10	4	10	8	8	4	10	7	9	6
♑	6	9	5	10	6	9	5	5	4	9	5	6
♒	9	6	10	5	9	5	9	7	9	5	9	3
♓	6	7	6	10	6	8	7	9	8	6	4	10

1 = the pits
10 = the peaks

Key

♈ – Aries
♉ – Taurus
♊ – Gemini
♋ – Cancer
♌ – Leo
♍ – Virgo

♎ – Libra
♏ – Scorpio
♐ – Sagittarius
♑ – Capricorn
♒ – Aquarius
♓ – Pisces

HOBBIES AND THE STARS

What do you do in your spare time? If you're looking for some new interests to keep you occupied in 2000, read on to discover which hobbies are ideal for your Sun sign.

 Libra

Libra is a very sensual sign, so any hobbies that appeal to your senses are bound to go down well. You love delicious smells so you might enjoy learning about aromatherapy, so you can cure yourself of minor ailments and also create your own bath oils. You could also get a big thrill out of making your own cosmetics or soaps, and you might become so good at them that you give them away as gifts. You take great pride in looking good, so you enjoy visiting your favourite shops and keeping up with the latest fashions. Music is one of your great loves and you might play an instrument or sing. If not, you certainly appreciate other people's musical talents and you enjoy going to concerts and recitals.

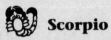 **Scorpio**

Whatever hobbies you choose, they have to mean a lot to you. You simply aren't interested in activities that don't carry an emotional meaning for you and you'd rather not bother with them at all. One pastime that's dear to the hearts of most Scorpios is wine-tasting. You might enjoy teaching yourself all about wine, either with the help of some good books or simply by drinking whatever appeals to you. You're fascinated by mysteries, and you could enjoy reading lots of whodunits or books on true crimes. You are also intrigued by things that go bump in the night, and you can't resist going on ghost hunts or visiting famous places that are known to be haunted.

Sagittarius

You're one of the great collectors of the zodiac, whether you know it or not. You may not think that you collect anything at all, but other people will take one look at all your books and beg to disagree with you. Reading is one of your great pleasures in life and you're always buying books on your latest enthusiasms. Travel is something else that appeals to you, and you love planning where you're going to go next on holiday. You like to keep active and you enjoy outdoor sports in particular. Horse-riding is a classic Sagittarian activity, and you enjoy going to the races and having a little flutter. You also like activities that present you with a challenge – you're always determined to beat it!

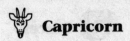 Capricorn

If you're a typical Capricorn you often take life rather seriously, so it's important for you to have lots of spare-time activities that allow you to relax. However, you've got to find the time first, and that means stopping work rather than burning the candle at both ends. Something that might appeal to you is rock-climbing, and you'll enjoy planning the strategy of how you're going to get to the top. Even a gentle walk amid mountain scenery does you a lot of good and helps you to relax. You're a very practical sign and you enjoy gardening. Not only does it help to ground you, you also like growing your own fruit and vegetables and then comparing the prices with those in the shops. Music helps you to unwind, and you'll love going to the opera or a glittering concert.

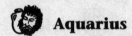 Aquarius

Most Aquarians have such a wide range of interests that almost anything is bound to appeal to you. You may go through phases, immersing yourself in one hobby for years until another one takes your fancy. However, you are only interested in activities that keep you intellectually stimulated and that teach you more about the world. You may go to lots of different evening classes, and you might even study for a degree in your spare time. Eastern philosophy could appeal, and you might also be an active campaigner for human rights. Astrology is a big hit with many Aquarians, and you'll enjoy teaching yourself all about it. Group activities are another interest, and you're an avid member of all sorts of organizations and societies.

Pisces

Anything artistic or creative is perfect for you, because you have abundant gifts at your disposal. Painting, drawing, writing poetry and dancing are all classic Piscean pastimes. In fact, you may feel rather fed up or stifled when you can't express yourself creatively. When you want to escape from the world, you love going to the cinema or the theatre. You're a Water sign so you enjoy any activities connected with water, such as swimming or other forms of water sports. Many Pisceans enjoy gardening, and you'll especially like having some form of water feature in your garden even if it's very modest. You're very musical, and would enjoy learning to play an instrument if you can't already do so. You might also like using your psychic talents, perhaps by learning to read the tarot or runes.

Aries

Ariens love to keep active, so you aren't interested in any sort of hobby that's very sedentary or that keeps you glued to the sofa. You much prefer being kept busy, especially if it's out of doors. You also have a strong sense of adventure and a great love of speed, so one hobby that's right up your street is motor-racing. You might be lucky enough to be the driver, or you could be a spectator shouting yourself hoarse from the stands, but this is a sport you love. Speaking of sports, anything that's competitive and which threatens to knock the stuffing out of you will also suit you down to the ground. Rugby, football and baseball all fit the bill, and you might also enjoy martial arts and Eastern forms of exercise such as T'ai Chi.

Taurus

You belong to one of the Earth signs, so it's no surprise that many Taureans were born with green fingers. You always feel better when you can be out in the fresh air, especially if you're in beautiful surroundings, so you adore gardening. Even if you're not keen on wielding a spade yourself you'll enjoy appreciating other people's efforts. Cooking is something that has enormous appeal for you and you enjoy creating gourmet meals, especially if the ingredients include your favourite foods. You also enjoy visiting swanky restaurants, although some of the gilt will be wiped off the gingerbread if you don't think you're getting value for money. Members of your sign are renowned for having beautiful voices so you might enjoy singing in a choir or on your own.

Gemini

One of your favourite ways of passing the time is to curl up with a good book. You'll eagerly read newspapers and magazines as well, and you always attempt crosswords and other sorts of puzzle even if you don't always finish them. Jigsaws intrigue you, especially if you can do something else at the same time, such as listening to music or watching the TV. You belong to a sign that doesn't like sitting still for long and you absolutely thrive on keeping active, so it's important for you to enjoy hobbies that make sure you get plenty of exercise. Tennis is a classic Gemini sport because it involves a lot of skill but it also boosts your social life. Dancing is another activity that helps you to keep fit while having a really good time.

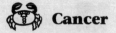 **Cancer**

Home comforts are very important to you, so you spend a lot of time and money on making sure your home is the way you want it. You may enjoy reading magazines on interior design or you could be glued to all the DIY programmes on TV, adapting the best ideas for your own home. One of your greatest skills is cooking, because you belong to a sign that derives enormous emotional comfort from food. You take pleasure in cooking for your loved ones and you probably have a big collection of cookery books to provide you with endless inspiration. Water sports could appeal to you, especially if they involve visiting your favourite beach. You might also enjoy fishing, particularly if you can do it by moonlight.

 Leo

You have a host of artistic skills and talents at your fingertips because you belong to the one of the most creative signs in the zodiac. One of your favourite hobbies is amateur dramatics, because most Leos adore being in the limelight. You may even have thought about becoming a professional actor because you enjoy treading the boards so much. You might also enjoy dancing, whether you go to regular classes or you simply love tripping the light fantastic with your partner. Travel appeals to you, especially if you can visit luxurious hotels in hot parts of the world. However, you're not very keen on roughing it! Clothes are very important to you, so you enjoy shopping for the latest fashions and you may also be an accomplished dressmaker.

Virgo

One of your favourite pastimes is to keep up to date with your health. You're fascinated by medical matters and you enjoy reading books telling you how to keep fit. You may even try out all the latest eating regimes, hoping that you'll find one that suits you perfectly. This interest in health means you're keen to eat well, and you could enjoy growing your own vegetables. Even cultivating a few herbs in a windowbox will give you a sense of achievement and you'll be pleased to think they are doing you good. You have tremendous patience so you might enjoy fiddly hobbies that require great dexterity, such as knitting, needlepoint and sewing. You might also enjoy painting designs on china and glass.

THE YEAR 2000

Friends and Lovers

If you're a typical Libran, relationships always mean a lot to you and you gain great satisfaction from other people's company. This year is no exception and you'll place a lot of importance on partnerships and loving links.

As the year begins, you're reaching the end of a very satisfying emotional phase that has continued from 1999. This has seen you establish stronger bonds with certain people in your life, and it may even have led to a new partnership. If you'd like to move in with someone or get married, the first six weeks of the year are a very auspicious time to make an emotional commitment.

After that, the picture changes and it's intimate relationships that will flourish. Your sex life looks very good between February and August. If you want to pep things up in the bedroom or get an intimate relationship off the ground, this is the time to do it.

There could be some big surprises in a loving relationship this year. You might see a new side to someone's personality or you may realize that they mean a lot more to you than you'd ever imagined. You could also fall for someone who's chalk to your cheese or who isn't your usual cup of tea at all, but who exerts a powerful attraction over you. It's second nature for you to put loved ones on pedestals, but try not to do this too often in 2000, otherwise you could be in for a big disappointment when you discover they're only human after all.

In January you might have to make an important decision about a friend, or you could meet someone who will turn out to play an important role in your life.

 **Health**

The best way to keep healthy this year is to make sure you have as much variety as possible in your life. Otherwise, you could quickly feel stagnant or bored. So it's a good idea to arrange lots of breaks and outings, so you've got plenty of things to look forward to. Ideally, you should get away on holiday to somewhere you've never been before because you'll love the sense of adventure. If you can go somewhere hot and exotic, so much the better!

You'll also enjoy good health if you can keep your brain active. You belong to one of the most intellectual signs in the zodiac and you certainly need to keep your mind busy in 2000. You could be interested in all sorts of ideas and activities, and some of them could be quite wacky. You won't mind one bit! You'll also enjoy expressing your artistic talents and these will help you to get the most out of life.

If you want to take more exercise in 2000 or find ways of keeping in trim, traditional outlets such as going to the gym could quickly lose their appeal. Instead, you'll much prefer getting into shape by doing something enjoyable, such as joining a dance class, doing some competitive running or doing underwater aerobics. You stand a much better chance of sticking with your chosen form of activity if you're having a good time while you do it. And if there's the chance of boosting your social life as well, you'll really be getting value for money!

Look after yourself in February and March, when you could feel slightly under par. You'll also be very susceptible to germs, so try to keep away from people who are obviously infectious. You will benefit from getting plenty of rest during this time, so it's the perfect opportunity to take off on holiday or to go away for a short break.

Money

Congratulations! After several years when money has been thin on the ground, at long last you're beginning to feel more flush. You may not yet be in the happy position of having money to burn, but at least you're feeling more confident about being able to keep the wolf from the door.

If you've got some spare money this year, think about how you can put it to good use. Should you salt it away in a pension plan, endowment policy or some other form of investment that will mature over the years? Playing the stock market could appeal to you, whether you do it by reading the financial pages or you rely on the help of a stockbroker. You'll love having a modest gamble with your money, especially between February and late June. You might also be very pleased when you make some inspired investments!

Nevertheless, it's not a year for taking risks that you can't afford, no matter how attractive they may seem. There will be times, especially between October and December, when it's best to be prudent and to save money rather than spend it. Seeking financial guidance is a good move between January and August, and you could receive some excellent advice. It may not be very adventurous but it will be very useful!

You'd be wise to stash away some money for a rainy day, especially if you rely on lots of gadgets and appliances. That's because something could go on the blink this year, such as a household appliance or your computer, and you'll need some readies in order to be able to fix it or, if the worst comes to the worst, to replace it.

Finally, if you fancy being extravagant, one wonderful way of spending money this year is to treat yourself to the holiday of a lifetime. If there's somewhere you've always wanted to visit, this is a terrific year to take off into the wide blue yonder.

 **Career**

Major changes have been affecting your daily routine over the past couple of years and that trend looks set to continue in 2000. You may alter your working surroundings in some way or you could switch jobs altogether. You might also find that you're spending more time working with the latest technology, or you have to learn a new skill in order to operate a computer or some other form of electronic appliance.

This is a fantastic year to go into partnership with someone. You'll find that two heads are definitely better than one, especially in the first six weeks of the year, and you'll enjoy bouncing ideas off one another. You may even have so much fun that you decide to make it a permanent arrangement! Between February and late June is the perfect time to pool your resources with someone, such as setting up in business with them or simply working with a colleague on a particular project.

It's also a wonderful year to make the most of your artistic abilities. If you don't already use your creative or artistic skills in the course of your career, think about how you can do this in 2000. Don't forget there are many ways of being creative, and what you should really be aiming at is using your innate skills and talents in ways that you enjoy. If your current job is more of a chore than anything else, perhaps it's time to look for something that gives you more scope and which isn't such an endurance test for you. Even the most modest beginnings could have some very exciting results.

Your Day by Day Guide

JANUARY AT A GLANCE

Love	♥ ♥ ♥ ♥ ♥
Money	£
Career	💻 💻 💻
Health	☼ ☼ ☼

• *Saturday 1 January* •

Happy New Year! You are feeling on top of the world today and full of optimism about the year ahead. You've got so much energy that you'll need to keep yourself busy doing things you enjoy and that are fun. Exercise would be a wonderful way of burning off not only any excess energy but also some of those extra calories you've probably acquired over the festive season.

• *Sunday 2 January* •

Your emotions are rather volatile today and you may find yourself acting on blind impulse and then wondering what you've got yourself into. You may feel a sudden attraction for someone and make a play for them, only to discover that you're not really keen on them after all. If you're already in an intimate relationship, you might blow hot and cold and not know how you really feel. Confusing!

• *Monday 3 January* •

If you're a typical Libran, relationships are your *raison d'être* and you spend a lot of time thinking about them. You'll have a particularly strong need today to openly display your affections, but the problem is that you're still in two minds about who you fancy! Remember that the grass always seems greener on the other side of the fence, and you could be setting yourself up for a fall.

• *Tuesday 4 January* •

Your capacity for insight into your emotions is heightened over the next five weeks, and you may well discover a part of your emotional make-up that you didn't know existed. See this as a golden opportunity, and don't be afraid to explore this new aspect of yourself. The more you know about what makes you tick, the less likely you are to be ambushed by difficult emotions.

• *Wednesday 5 January* •

If you took the plunge and analysed yourself yesterday, you will be pleased to know that you'll start to reap the benefits today. You'll feel much more in tune with yourself and you'll be able to communicate your feelings with clarity and honesty. This bodes well for an intimate relationship because at last you will both know where you stand.

• *Thursday 6 January* •

Today's New Moon gives you the opportunity of establishing a stronger and more secure foundation to your life during the coming fortnight. Your home base will start to become more important to you and this is an excellent time to begin any constructive changes that need to be made. You'll also start to feel an increasing sense of inner fulfilment.

• *Friday 7 January* •

You are in a very easy-going mood today and your famous Libran charm will have others eating out of your hand. A love affair could really start to blossom, especially if you've been through a rocky patch recently. Your caring and supportive qualities are very apparent, and you're willing to lend a sympathetic ear and do whatever you can to help someone in need.

• Saturday 8 January •

Even the best-laid plans could go up in smoke today so you'll need to be as flexible as possible. Funnily enough, this will turn out to be to your advantage because whatever you end up doing may be more enjoyable than what you originally had in mind. Once you allow yourself to go with the flow, all sorts of unexpected and wonderful things could happen.

• Sunday 9 January •

A conversation between you and a certain someone will really affect you today, and it will bring home to you just how much you value the relationship. Perhaps you have never experienced such powerful feelings for someone before and you are feeling slightly overwhelmed by this realization? The power of love is about to transform you and change your preconceived ideas forever.

• Monday 10 January •

Keep your eyes and ears open today because you could be offered a very special opportunity that you would hate to miss. You might get the chance to change the way you work for the better, or you may be able to prove your worth to your colleagues. This is also a good day to incorporate some kind of exercise routine into your daily life – you'll feel a lot more energetic if you do.

• Tuesday 11 January •

If you're not careful your emotions could take a battering today because someone close to home has about as much sensitivity as a scrubbing brush. Do they have an axe to grind or are they totally unaware of the impact their comments make on other people? Either way, you'd do well to protect yourself by trying to avoid getting into a serious conversation with them.

• *Wednesday 12 January* •

A strong urge to spend money takes you over today, and you'll be in the mood to treat yourself to some little luxuries. Anything that enhances the way you look and feel would be worth spending money on, so you might fancy a relaxing massage or a facial with aromatherapy oils. Whatever you do, the accent is on pleasure and giving yourself what you deserve.

• *Thursday 13 January* •

If you're in the thick of an intense love affair, this will be a day to remember because you will be swept off your feet by some intoxicating feelings. You're in love with love at the moment and you're enjoying every minute of it – and what Libran wouldn't! Whether it lasts for a week or a lifetime, you're determined to squeeze every romantic minute from it that you can.

• *Friday 14 January* •

Communications could go a little haywire today so be prepared for letters and messages to go astray or misunderstandings between you and others. Take extra care in everything you say to avoid someone getting the wrong end of the stick, and watch your temper because you'll feel very impatient and frustrated if anything goes wrong.

• *Saturday 15 January* •

It is difficult to understand what a loved one wants from you today, and they may not have much idea themselves! They could be in a dreamy state or they might become confused about something. Try to take it in your stride because it won't last long. If you want to relax, you will love curling up with a good book or watching a favourite film, preferably in some very cosy company.

• *Sunday 16 January* •

You long to keep the home fires burning today and you don't want to wander too far afield. You're in a busy and productive mood, so if you've got any DIY to do or you feel like having a bit of a clear-out, this is the ideal day to do it. Once you get going, there'll be no stopping you until you've got everything in perfect order. You might come across an old photo or souvenir that makes you feel really nostalgic for the past.

• *Monday 17 January* •

You've still got plenty of energy today and you'll want to finish off what you started yesterday before you make any other plans. You're not in a particularly frivolous or sociable mood and you'd far rather do something challenging that stretches you both physically and mentally. If you run your own business, you might put in some extra hours to keep ahead.

• *Tuesday 18 January* •

Your appetite for life is limitless during the coming fortnight and you'll want to pack as much as you can into your days. You will be in the mood for adventure and the last thing you will want is to be stuck in a routine. Your mind is working very creatively now and you could come up with a scheme or idea that will give you greater freedom in your life. Sounds promising!

• *Wednesday 19 January* •

For the next couple of weeks your thoughts will be turning to how to make your life more interesting and rewarding. If there's a part of you that no longer feels happy in your personal or professional life, start thinking about what it is you'd really like to change. The more dissatisfied you are, the more motivated you will be to improve matters now.

• *Thursday 20 January* •

You're charm personified today, making it easy for you to get along with everyone around you. You'll feel like being with your favourite people, doing what you love the most, because anything that smacks of hard work will be too much effort. If you're in a position to indulge your vision of a perfect day, you'll be in seventh heaven. If not, you can always try again another day!

• *Friday 21 January* •

Today's Full Moon could make you extremely sensitive to criticism during the coming fortnight, and you may find yourself overreacting out of a false sense of pride. It would be better not to try to get to grips with how you're feeling just yet because you lack perspective at the moment. There could be a tug of war between how you want to be and what others expect of you.

• *Saturday 22 January* •

Although Librans love being in a relationship, your main priority today is gaining some emotional independence for yourself. You could feel rather hemmed in and restricted, and even if a certain someone feels perfectly justified in their behaviour, you experience them as being too demanding. It's time to ask yourself what it is you really want.

• *Sunday 23 January* •

You're very wrapped up in your own thoughts today and you'll probably want to be left alone to make a few decisions. Your thinking is cool and rational, and you're much less likely to be swayed by your emotions when considering your various options. This could affect your feelings for a certain person but, if so, will this change of heart last long?

• *Monday 24 January* •

Expand your horizons today and do something that you haven't tried before. You're in the mood to delight your senses and have your eyes opened to something new. For example, you could go to an exotic restaurant and taste a completely different kind of food, or you might visit a place that you've always felt drawn to. Whatever you choose to do, your life will be enriched as a result.

• *Tuesday 25 January* •

Your emotions and thoughts are working at cross purposes today, and to say that you feel confused would be an understatement. You may decide to keep your confusion to yourself because, apart from anything else, it would be really hard to put anything into words at this stage. On the other hand, using someone as a sounding board could help to clarify things. Decisions, decisions!

• *Wednesday 26 January* •

You'll be focusing on home and family matters for the next few weeks and seeing how you can improve the status quo. On a physical level, you may want to make some structural changes that will enhance your comfort. On an emotional level, it might be a good idea to have a family meeting so that everyone can air their grievances and make some positive suggestions about how to create a more harmonious atmosphere.

• *Thursday 27 January* •

Think big today because you're in the mood for making sweeping changes and not doing anything by half-measures. You can achieve a lot more than usual, especially if you want to patch up things with a partner or loved one. If there are any other areas in your life where you want to go for broke, make sure you know what you're doing rather than simply relying on luck.

• *Friday 28 January* •

Be very careful if you're involved in any kind of negotiations or agreements today because you could end up losing out. Double-check the small print before you commit yourself to anything, and if you get a sneaky feeling that you might be making a mistake, quit while you're still ahead. Someone you thought you could trust may turn out to be a lot less reliable than you imagined.

• *Saturday 29 January* •

If you've had to put your social life on the back burner for a while, don't worry because it starts to go full steam ahead again today. Ideally, you should seek out some mentally stimulating company and people who can talk to you in interesting and witty ways. You'll get bored easily so anyone who doesn't engage you will quickly lose your attention. Try not to inadvertently hurt someone's feelings.

• *Sunday 30 January* •

You're not in the most tolerant of moods today and someone close to home could easily put your back up over a personal issue. Normally you might chose to grit your teeth and ignore it, but this time you'll find it almost impossible to keep quiet. One word of warning – choose your words carefully because you may come across as overly critical and therefore will exacerbate the problem.

• *Monday 31 January* •

If you can be honest with yourself about your feelings, you'll be able to move forward and know in your heart that you're doing what is best for you. A good long talk with a friend who you trust and respect will help you to sort out the wheat from the chaff and come to terms with how things really are, rather than how you would like them to be.

FEBRUARY AT A GLANCE

Love	♥ ♥ ♥ ♥ ♥
Money	£ $ £ $
Career	💻 💻 💻 💻 💻
Health	☼ ☼ ☼ ☼ ☼

• *Tuesday 1 February* •

You have the courage of your convictions today and you certainly won't be pulling your punches in your dealings with others. Your current desire to go straight to the heart of the issue will help you to clear up any confusion or misunderstandings with a partner or loved one – it will make all the difference. If you have to give a talk, presentation or sell yourself in some way, you'll make quite an impact.

• *Wednesday 2 February* •

Your confidence alone will help you to sail through today and, even though you might have been wary of picking up the gauntlet before, you now feel ready to tackle life head on. Fortunately, you've got lots of support from the people who count and, with everyone rooting for you, there's really no stopping you from reaching your goals.

• *Thursday 3 February* •

If you've been meaning to have a brainstorming session with someone, this is a good day to do it. You may have some domestic finances to sort out and, on a broader level, you may also need to iron out issues connected with shared resources and who pays for what. If you feel you have a better grip on these matters than you-know-who, don't be afraid to assert yourself.

• *Friday 4 February* •

Good news! You could have a lucky break today which opens a new door and offers you a golden opportunity. You'll just happen to be in the right place at the right time, and you could meet someone who will be instrumental in helping you to move forward. If you think of this person as a kind of guardian angel you won't be far wrong. So get ready to count your blessings!

• *Saturday 5 February* •

Today's New Moon provides you with the opportunity over the next few weeks to start a new venture or project that will earn you more recognition and boost your self-esteem. You probably already have plenty of ideas, and all you need to do now is to put your plan into action and watch it develop. It's time for you to shine more brightly and to create something really worthwhile.

• *Sunday 6 February* •

You're a real live wire today! You're so full of beans and you'll want it to stay that way because you have a hectic schedule ahead. You've got your own agenda and you'll need to be as unhampered as possible if you are going to get everything done. Any attempt to tie you down will not be appreciated, so you had better warn all concerned to give you plenty of space.

• *Monday 7 February* •

If someone at work is beginning to drain you or get you down, this is a good time to broach the subject with them and see if there's anything you can both do to create a better working environment. Perhaps they're depressed without really knowing it, in which case they need to become aware of how their suppressed feelings are affecting other people. Try to get them to talk.

• *Tuesday 8 February* •

The more predictable or boring your routine is today, the more you'll want to scream with frustration. The trouble is that things aren't moving fast enough for you and you're finding it hard to be patient. There are lots of jobs to do now that will totally absorb you if you're willing to buckle down and apply yourself. Think of it as a means to an end.

• *Wednesday 9 February* •

You can breathe a sigh of relief today because life looks much more exciting than it did yesterday. Ideally, you should grab the chance to branch out in new directions and to acquire the taste for something completely different. If you have the opportunity to meet some new people, jump at it because you might meet someone who complements your *joie de vivre* perfectly.

• *Thursday 10 February* •

You're in a dilemma as to whether to play it safe or take a risk today. Part of you wants to stay with what you know and maintain the status quo, while another part of you feels inspired to take a leap into the unknown. If you think things over, you may discover that it's not a case of having to choose, because you can incorporate both the old and the new into your life.

• *Friday 11 February* •

Don't delay if you need to sort out your accounts or work out a budget, because you're in a very practical and money-minded mood. You're feeling very assertive and you won't have any difficulties in chasing up any money owed to you or solving a financial mystery. If you're thinking of committing yourself to a major expenditure, you'll know exactly how much money you've got to play with.

• *Saturday 12 February* •

Relationships will be highlighted during the coming six weeks. You will feel a lot more determined to stand up for yourself than usual, and as a result there could be a few run-ins with a partner. This could be a good thing if you usually believe in anything for a quiet life. However, try to resist the temptation to have a good old shouting match simply for the sake of it.

• *Sunday 13 February* •

You will feel like getting as far away as possible today from your everyday life and having a sociable time in a totally new and stimulating environment. If you can get together with a group of your favourite people and do something fun and out of the ordinary, you'll have the recipe for a perfect day out. Enjoy yourself!

• *Monday 14 February* •

Happy Valentine's Day! If this is one of the most important days in your calendar, you won't be disappointed. If you're currently a solo Libra, you could experience a powerful and hypnotic attraction to someone. Once you get talking to them, you will feel as if you've always known them. If you are already in a relationship, get set to deepen your commitment now.

• *Tuesday 15 February* •

If you're a true Libran, you are extremely fair-minded, and before jumping to conclusions you always do your best to consider all sides of an argument. These qualities will stand you in good stead today because someone will expect you to give a balanced appraisal of a situation. This could win you a lot of approval (something you're not averse to) and will mean you are even more in demand. Lucky you!

• *Wednesday 16 February* •

Keeping everyone happy is often the role that Librans choose for themselves, and never more so than today. It seems that you want to take care of everyone's needs and you'll act like a magnet for anyone who wants to unburden themselves. While you may feel that you're doing everyone a lot of good by being so available, you don't want them to become too dependent on you. Help them to help themselves.

• *Thursday 17 February* •

Your emotions are extra sensitive today, making you feel quite vulnerable at times. As a result, you might want to retreat into your shell and not come out until you feel strong again. The trouble is that you probably won't get a chance to hide away because there's a situation at work that means you are very much on show and in the limelight. Try to protect yourself as best you can.

• *Friday 18 February* •

You are rather unfocused today and you might be trying to escape life's harsh realities by retreating into your fantasy world. It's important that you acknowledge how you really feel rather than disown any negative emotions you might have, otherwise these will catch you out later on. A partner will be sympathetic and considerate.

• *Saturday 19 February* •

Is something worrying you at the moment? If you feel that your life isn't your own because it's been taken over by certain anxieties or cares, over the coming fortnight you will get the chance to do something about it. This may involve pouring your heart out to someone or seeking their advice. Alternatively, you may feel brave enough to face up to what is wrong and decide how you can fix it.

• *Sunday 20 February* •

Something could happen today that restores your faith in life and makes you feel so much more positive about everything. If you felt as though you'd lost your sense of humour, don't worry because it's back with a vengeance. In fact, having a good laugh about something is the perfect antidote to the recent setbacks you've suffered. You will feel renewed and in good spirits.

• *Monday 21 February* •

Life is full of interesting challenges today, and the more you mix with people who give you something to think about, the happier you'll be. You will naturally gravitate towards those who share your open-mindedness because you would rather learn something new about yourself than simply stick with what you already know. It's a time of self-discovery.

• *Tuesday 22 February* •

You've got stars in your eyes today, and that can only mean one thing! Yes, you're in a wonderfully romantic and idealistic mood, making it almost impossible for you to admit that a certain person has a single flaw. However divine you believe them to be, don't forget that they are only human. If you blind yourself to that truth you could be setting yourself up for a fall.

• *Wednesday 23 February* •

Today you discover the truth about the saying that a problem shared is a problem halved. Talking things through will bring you closer to the person you confide in. In fact, you shouldn't do anything alone today because you'll particularly enjoy the company of friends and loved ones. If you're in a creative field, you will feel strongly inspired to work in a new and imaginative way, and what you produce will attract a lot of positive attention.

• *Thursday 24 February* •

Life is for living today, and you are determined to enjoy yourself whenever you get the chance. Unfortunately, work or other chores could get in the way but you will tackle them with a good grace. As a bonus, you will find it easy to get on well with colleagues and workmates. It's a great day to buy something that will boost your health or make you feel like a million dollars.

• *Friday 25 February* •

Someone close to home has a hankering for emotional freedom today and it's causing all sorts of mixed reactions in you. You might be surprised to discover a strongly jealous streak that you didn't know you possessed and which threatens to wreak havoc unless you can keep it under control. Try to talk about how you're really feeling rather than pretend that everything is absolutely fine.

• *Saturday 26 February* •

If you've managed to negotiate some fairly choppy waters recently you will be relieved to know that you feel on much more solid ground today. Yesterday's rather broody mood gives way to a much more light-hearted frame of mind, and you can have some very constructive talks with a loved one about the way you feel things are going for you at the moment.

• *Sunday 27 February* •

Life gets better and better today and you feel really lively, sociable and energetic. You're determined to have as much fun as possible and you might even have a light-hearted flirtation with someone and feel good about it. You're not in the mood for anything too intense, and you'll be happiest if you give yourself room to breathe.

• *Monday 28 February* •

Is someone spoiling for a fight? A neighbour or sibling could prove to be rather awkward today and even your diplomatic skills won't be enough to prevent a heated exchange. Exactly why they are being so demanding and difficult is hard to fathom because they're not exactly being coherent. You may be forced to bite the bullet and have it out with them.

• *Tuesday 29 February* •

Try to introduce as much variation into your day as possible because you'll quickly get bored and restless if you have to stay too long in one place. If you're at work, try to set yourself a challenge or deadline because you'll work better if you're under pressure. If a relationship has felt stagnant recently, you might be tempted to throw a stick of dynamite under you-know-who.

MARCH AT A GLANCE

Love	♥ ♥ ♥
Money	£ $ £ $
Career	💻 💻 💻 💻 💻
Health	☼ ☼ ☼ ☼ ☼

• *Wednesday 1 March* •

You are a better talker than listener today, which could have both advantages and disadvantages. On the positive side, you'll be able to express yourself with confidence and ease and say what you mean without hurting anyone's feelings. On the negative side, someone might really need to get something off their chest and they will feel they can't get a word in edgeways.

• *Thursday 2 March* •

If you have been faced with some health concerns for a while now, and conventional medicine hasn't been able to help, why not give some alternative therapies a try? A more holistic approach may be more helpful and give you a clearer picture of what's causing any symptoms you might have. Take a look at your diet and lifestyle, and see if there's room for improvement.

• *Friday 3 March* •

Not for nothing are you called the charmer of the zodiac, and you'll enhance this reputation today with great success. Not only will you dazzle others with your wit and lively conversation, you could have a powerful effect on someone who instantly falls under your spell. You will have to proceed with caution unless you happen to be a free agent.

• *Saturday 4 March* •

You are determined not to let the grass grow under your feet today, and you'll pack as much as you can into your day. If you're planning on going shopping you could make lots of impulse buys when all sorts of interesting things catch your eye, so be prepared to spend more than you might have budgeted for. You could receive a surprise gift from an anonymous admirer. Sounds intriguing!

• *Sunday 5 March* •

If you got a little carried away on your shopping spree yesterday, you might not dare to check your finances today to see how much damage has been done. In actual fact, you're probably feeling fairly relaxed and philosophical about the state of your finances and confident that the money is coming in. You could have a tendency to over-indulge on food today, so take note if you're watching your waistline!

• *Monday 6 March* •

Over the coming fortnight you need to assess your current work situation. Is everything going OK or are you fed up with the way things are going at the moment? If you have been wondering about finding a new job, this is the perfect time to start looking. It will also be a very favourable time to improve your relationship with certain colleagues or customers, especially if they are often a pain in the neck.

• *Tuesday 7 March* •

If you're a true Libran, you probably spend considerable amounts of time sitting on the fence trying to make up your mind. Well, get set to act out of character today because you're in a very forthright and direct mood, and you are not prepared to waste time by beating about the bush. In fact, a loved one or partner is about to be hit right between the eyes!

• *Wednesday 8 March* •

If you have been trying to find the words to broach a difficult subject, now is the time to take the bull by the horns and say what you really think. You'll find that the words just flow, and however awkward or embarrassing the situation is, the other person will react in a more positive way than you think. The more honest you are, the easier it will be to clear the air.

• *Thursday 9 March* •

Have you got your nose to the grindstone? You have a strong sense of commitment and duty today, and you'll take everything you do very seriously. If you have a job to complete, you will stick with it until you've finished – even if it interferes with your social life. It's more important to you right now to feel you've achieved something worthwhile.

• *Friday 10 March* •

You need to focus on your emotional and financial security today and reassess how important these are to you. On a practical level, you may need to sort out any joint financial arrangement that you have with a partner or loved one and see how well it's working for you both. Make any adjustments that are necessary now before a difference of opinion turns into a power struggle.

• *Saturday 11 March* •

Your thoughts take a very romantic and sentimental turn today. You could find yourself falling in love with you-know-who all over again or you could be smitten by someone you have only just met. Whether it's a new love or an old one, your whole world is coloured by feelings of happiness and contentment now. If you fancy having a last-minute weekend break, choose an idyllic setting.

• *Sunday 12 March* •

You feel very positive about the direction your life is heading in right now and you can relax in the certain knowledge that everything is unfolding according to plan. As a result, you can enjoy life to the full today and do whatever takes your fancy, especially if it means breaking with your usual Sunday routine and trying something new.

• *Monday 13 March* •

You're determined to turn over a new leaf today and make some significant changes in your life over the next few weeks. If you've been thinking of giving up smoking or drinking but have not found the willpower to do it, you can now draw on the strength you need to kick the habit. You're looking at yourself in a new light and are ready to let go of the old you.

• *Tuesday 14 March* •

Things are really starting to move on the career front and today you feel very confident about your ability to handle all the positive changes that are coming your way. Start thinking about different ways of how you can put your name on the map and get a plan of action together. You'll be surprised at how much help and support there is for you to draw on – don't ignore it.

• *Wednesday 15 March* •

Are you planning a family reunion? Being with loved ones will give you a lot of pleasure today, especially if you can all go out and do something you enjoy together. You're in the mood for saying how much you care, and you'll want to back it up with lots of affectionate hugs and kisses. Librans are never happier than when harmony reigns supreme, so it looks as though you'll be in your element.

• *Thursday 16 March* •

If you've been rather extravagant recently and have been finding it hard to keep a firm control on your finances, this is an excellent time to go through your bank statements and credit card bills and assess the situation. You might decide to cut back on your expenses for a while just to get back on an even keel, or you may think up a plan to earn more money.

• *Friday 17 March* •

Someone might try to muscle in on you today and make you feel as though you belong to them, which you won't like one bit. This could be a person who has admired you from afar and suddenly feels that they own you, or it could be a partner who's trying to hold on to you a little too tightly. Either way, you'll let them know in no uncertain terms that you're not amused by their behaviour.

• *Saturday 18 March* •

You will instinctively adopt a positive attitude to everything you do today and you'll take pleasure in even the simplest things. Even the mundane rituals that you do every weekend will seem rather reassuring and comforting, and you'll be happy to get on with any chores around the house or in the garden. Familiarity breeds contentment today.

• *Sunday 19 March* •

If you've been plucking up the courage to do something that requires daring and initiative, then there's no time like the present to overcome your fears and take the plunge. Whether what you have to say is a declaration of love or war, you'll be more confident than you imagine once you've made up your mind to come clean. One thing's for sure, things will change considerably after that.

• *Monday 20 March* •

Be prepared to begin the day feeling tense as a result of today's Full Moon. If you realize that you're rather tired or fraught, try to take it easy, otherwise your emotions could get the better of you and the rest of the day will be an uphill struggle. You might easily get into a state about things that you normally take in your stride, so don't be too hard on yourself.

• *Tuesday 21 March* •

Yesterday's rather stressful quality has disappeared, leaving you feeling able to deal with anything that comes your way. Not that you have anything to worry about because it promises to be an excellent day, particularly if you're trying to make progress at work. If you're involved in a project that allows you to develop your talents and skills, you'll come on in leaps and bounds.

• *Wednesday 22 March* •

Although as a Libran you love to keep other people happy, you do have to stand up for yourself at times and risk incurring someone's wrath. This is one of those days when you're torn between keeping the peace and giving you-know-who a piece of your mind. Don't give them the upper hand by showing that you're afraid of causing a scene, as this won't do your relationship any favours and will only weaken your self-esteem.

• *Thursday 23 March* •

Your bark may be worse than your bite during the next few weeks, but at least it will let others know that you're not a complete push-over. You can let off steam today without having a full-scale row, and get a lot of hidden tension and resentment out in the open. Showing a certain someone that you have a mind of your own, and are not afraid to use it, will do wonders for your self-confidence and redress the balance of power.

• *Friday 24 March* •

You may be tempted to break with tradition today and do something unconventional or unusual. Perhaps you've had a change of attitude recently and it's made you question a lot of your ideas and ideals, so you wonder how realistic they really are. Before you throw out the baby with the bathwater, give yourself a period of time to decide what you still believe in.

• *Saturday 25 March* •

The next few weeks will bring renewed vigour and increased emotional and physical stamina into your life. You'll be much more willing than usual to confront situations that you aren't happy with, and both personal and professional partnerships will undergo a major overhaul. As you will be initiating all these changes, you'll have a strong sense of being able to direct the course of your own life. Congratulations!

• *Sunday 26 March* •

Is your loyalty to certain people well-founded or misplaced? The planets are encouraging you to look at your life and your relationships with greater realism so that you can gain a truer perspective on everything. It could be that you've been putting someone on a pedestal but, at the same time, undervaluing yourself and not recognizing your full worth. It's never too late to change!

• *Monday 27 March* •

Are you ready to enhance your reputation? If you've been working on your self-image recently, you'll be pleased to know that what you project today will impress more than a few key people. A situation at work could show up your innate skills as a mediator, and a boss or superior will admire your ability to bring out the best in people, especially any bright ideas they might have. Well done!

• *Tuesday 28 March* •

You could be in the mood to do some cleaning today and you'll want to give the house a face-lift from top to bottom. If you've accumulated a lot of clutter over the past few months, now is the time to have a good clear-out. If you are feeling really energetic, you might even tackle some decorating. You'll be amazed by how much it will boost your morale.

• *Wednesday 29 March* •

Don't dismiss an opportunity that comes your way today on the grounds that it doesn't seem to offer much. Once you start to investigate it more thoroughly, you will discover that it holds a lot more promise than you thought. The same goes for someone you meet who doesn't seem to match up to your expectations, but who definitely has hidden potential. Watch this space!

• Thursday 30 March •

Are you ready for someone to get up close and personal? If you have had a secret yearning for a certain person and was about to give up on anything ever happening – don't! This person could come into your orbit with a vengeance today and leave you feeling slightly breathless. Whether this proves to be simply a flirtation, or a longer-lasting liaison, it will leave an indelible mark.

• Friday 31 March •

You'll want to achieve your personal best today and you'll make great efforts to forge ahead at work or in anything else to which you are deeply committed. You ooze confidence, and you'll have no difficulties putting yourself forward for a new job or a promotion or simply speaking up for yourself. You could get a lot of satisfaction from helping someone further their ambitions.

APRIL AT A GLANCE

Love	♥ ♥ ♥ ♥ ♥
Money	£ $ £ $ £
Career	💻 💻 💻
Health	☼ ☼ ☼

• Saturday 1 April •

You need to get your teeth into something today and you should make the most of your energy levels because if you plan your time well, you'll get everything done that you wanted to and more. With luck, what you have in mind will be more of a joy than a chore, but even if you do have to tackle something demanding, your positive attitude will make it enjoyable.

• Sunday 2 April •

You are very sensitive to someone's feelings today and you'll offer them whatever support they need at this time. Perhaps they've recently been ill or suffered a loss and they need some cheering up or simply a sympathetic ear. Either way, you'll be happy to give them plenty of time and input and to let them know they're not alone. If you feel tired or worn out by the end of the day, do something nice for yourself. You will deserve it!

• Monday 3 April •

You feel like spreading your wings today and leaving your everyday world behind for a while. This would be an ideal day to start planning a holiday and getting some brochures together. You're probably more in the mood for something adventurous, but if you will be travelling with someone who prefers to play it safe, you'll have to use all your charm to bring them round to what you have in mind. A piece of cake!

• Tuesday 4 April •

You're feeling very amorous over the coming fortnight, and if you meet someone you fancy you certainly won't be backwards in coming forwards! You shouldn't blame this person for thinking that you only want them for one thing because the animal magnetism you're exuding should be X-rated! If you've already got a partner, the passion between you will be unleashed in full force. Wow!

• *Wednesday 5 April* •

It may be rather hard to turn your attention to work today but unless you do, you'll find that you go off the boil altogether. You'll have to muster all the self-discipline you can, and even if you're simply going through the motions at least you will look as if you're doing what you're supposed to. Try to get out for a walk to clear your head and bring you back down to earth.

• *Thursday 6 April* •

You'll be touched by someone's kindness and generosity of spirit today, and if you needed to restore your faith in human nature this will do the trick. If a partner or loved one has been holding back emotionally recently, they will be much more forthcoming over the next few weeks, and you'll be able to share your feelings and establish a deeper rapport.

• *Friday 7 April* •

If you've got a problem to solve today, the best way to deal with it is to face up to it and tackle it head on. Fortunately, you don't have to do battle on your own as you have all the emotional support and psychological back-up that you need from someone close to home. You will soon discover that once you confront your fears they won't seem nearly so overwhelming as they first appeared.

• *Saturday 8 April* •

You are full of beans today, and the more activities you can involve yourself in the better. You will need frequent changes of scene to stave off any boredom and you'll positively thrive on lots of company, especially if there's something exciting you can all do. Try to get as much exercise as possible to burn

off all that nervous energy, otherwise you might get hyper-
active and go OTT!

• *Sunday 9 April* •

You're still brimming with energy and vitality today, which
means that you'll want to keep active and enjoy yourself as
much as possible. Your powers of attraction are particularly
strong and you'll make a lasting impression on anyone new
that you meet. If you're currently single, destiny could be
about to orchestrate a fated encounter. Keep your eyes peeled!

• *Monday 10 April* •

If you thought that someone had reneged on a promise they'd
made to you, you'll be glad to know that they'll come up
trumps today. This means that you can now get on with a
project or plan that you've been waiting to put into action for
some time and that will improve your status in some way.
Once everything starts to move, you could find that a piece of
luck arrives from out of the blue to help things along.

• *Tuesday 11 April* •

You're in a very conscientious mood today and you'll be
working all hours to get ahead of your workload. This may
cause some friction between you and a certain someone who
would like to spend more time with you than you have
available. Having to pass up on your social life doesn't exactly
make you happy either, but you have to prioritize and, right
now, work comes first.

• *Wednesday 12 April* •

You won't regret having put your career ahead of everything
else recently because you'll reap the rewards of your investment today. You have reached some kind of pinnacle and

you'll be rewarded for your efforts by being given the praise you deserve. Not only is this very gratifying to your ego, you'll find it emotionally fulfilling as well.

• *Thursday 13 April* •

Be prepared to compromise during the rest of the month, but make sure that you say what you think and you put across your point of view. If you can manage to voice your emotions you'll gain a lot from talking to someone who's sympathetic but objective, and who can help you to come to terms with how you're feeling. Learning more about how you function emotionally will be very beneficial for you now.

• *Friday 14 April* •

You may inadvertently arouse a partner's antagonism today by saying or doing the wrong thing. Perhaps there have been some hidden tensions between you and what happens today is the straw that breaks the camel's back. Potential causes for a row are joint money matters, jealousy or sexual problems, and although you may not want to open up cans of worms like those, it is important to clear the air and get your feelings out into the open.

• *Saturday 15 April* •

The next few weeks favour communication of all kinds and you're likely to meet lots of new and interesting people in both your personal and professional life. You could meet someone today with whom you have a strong intellectual rapport, and before you know it you'll have become firm friends. Don't be surprised if they open up a whole new world to you.

• *Sunday 16 April* •

This is a marvellous day to join forces with either one person or a group of people and to do something you really enjoy.

You're in the mood for fun and companionship, and if you feel like spreading your wings, why not take off for the day and expand your horizons. You could find yourself drawing closer to someone who's always been a bit of an enigma to you.

• Monday 17 April •

You feel truly blessed with friends and loved ones today and you'll want to spend time with some of your favourite people. Never one to shy away from a social gathering, you'll lap up every enjoyable minute with those you love and can be completely yourself with. If you feel like telling someone how much they mean to you, don't hold back because it will mean the world to them.

• Tuesday 18 April •

If you have to choose between business and pleasure today, there's no doubt what your decision would be. You're in the mood to have a good time but, if you do have to work, you will make the best of it and your constructive attitude will ensure that the day goes well. You could have an interesting chat with a boss or authority figure that makes you see them in a more positive light.

• Wednesday 19 April •

The current Full Moon will raise some important questions about your life over the next fortnight. You might realize that certain associations or arrangements no longer suit you or have a place in your world. If a project or venture has been floundering recently, this is when you can decide whether to battle on or whether it would be better to cut your losses and start again from scratch.

• *Thursday 20 April* •

Take care today because a close partner could spring some tricky surprises on you. They may long to have more emotional freedom than they do at the moment, and as a result they may want to do their own thing or go their own sweet way. This may only be a temporary state of affairs but you could feel thrown or hurt by it. A child or adolescent may also want to kick against the traces today.

• *Friday 21 April* •

This is an ideal time to take off into the wide blue yonder for a long weekend. You have a strong desire to travel and visit new places, and even if you can't go very far afield you'll be glad you made the effort to get away. Whatever your destination, there's a strong likelihood that you will fall in love with the place and not want to come back.

• *Saturday 22 April* •

You are filled with tremendous conviction today, and if you need to convert someone to your way of thinking your powers of persuasion will win the day. It's not simply that you happen to believe something is true, you feel totally passionate about it and that's what will appeal to other people. Don't underestimate the impact you have on others now – it's explosive!

• *Sunday 23 April* •

If someone voices an opinion that you consider to be narrow-minded or upsetting to others, you'll have no hesitation in challenging them and taking them to task. Whereas before you might have considered it politic to keep a dignified silence, this time you feel too strongly about the issues at stake and you would rather run the risk of being unpopular than denying your true feelings.

• *Monday 24 April* •

If you've got an important decision to make concerning someone's welfare, make sure you weigh up all the considerations before reaching a conclusion. It could be that a relative needs extra care and you have to decide what's best for them, or you may have to think of a child's education and which school will suit them best. Talk it over with someone you trust and respect.

• *Tuesday 25 April* •

Your love life hasn't always been exactly a bed of roses but you can be sure that today promises a wonderful mixture of romance and passion. This will prove to be a deliciously exotic cocktail, breathing new life into your partnership and giving you the confirmation you needed that what you have is still worth fighting for.

• *Wednesday 26 April* •

Do yourself a favour and steer clear of anyone who's likely to criticize you or try to take you down a peg or two. You're feeling rather sensitive today and, whereas you might normally laugh something off, if you had to endure someone's caustic humour now they would probably reduce you to tears. Come to think of it, perhaps it's time that you started avoiding them for good?

• *Thursday 27 April* •

Friendships are of prime importance today and you will feel able to count on different people for all the support you need. You will feel well off both emotionally and materially. If you are going out on the town, consider visiting somewhere that you have never tried before or which is often too unconventional for you. It will have a strong appeal for you now.

• *Friday 28 April* •

If you are aware that you need to discuss certain issues with you-know-who, this is an excellent day to start. You will be able to choose your words carefully yet still say what is on your mind. You could have a very interesting and valuable discussion! If you've got your heart set on someone but you don't know if they have even noticed you properly, try to engineer a way of breaking the ice today. The results could make you feel all warm inside!

• *Saturday 29 April* •

You are feeling very industrious today and you'll throw yourself into any chores that need doing around the house. Establishing a routine for your day will be very therapeutic, giving you a sense of peace and order. It will also give you time to think. If you have been worried about a health problem or work difficulty, what happens today could set your mind at rest.

• *Sunday 30 April* •

You enter a time of soul-searching from today, and over the coming fortnight you will benefit in many ways from examining your heart and the current state of your emotions. You may ask yourself why certain people are still in your life or whether a close partner gives you the satisfaction and support that you need from your relationship. You might even ask yourself whether you fulfil the needs of the people in your life. If not, how can you improve the situation?

MAY AT A GLANCE

Love	♥ ♥ ♥
Money	£ $ £ $ £
Career	💻 💻 💻
Health	☼

• Monday 1 May •

Don't know whether you're coming or going? You will be prone to scattering your energies today so you won't get a lot done, despite the fact that you'll probably be working flat out for most of the day. Rather than doing three things at once, decide what's most important and focus on that to the exclusion of everything else – you'll be a lot more productive. It will be more satisfying to do one thing well than lots of things badly.

• Tuesday 2 May •

You won't know what's got into a loved one today and the more you try to please and placate them, the more difficult and contrary they seem to be. Your best bet is to leave them to stew and hope that they'll eventually come around and start acting like a civilized human being again. In the meantime, do something nice for yourself that makes you feel good.

• Wednesday 3 May •

Just when you thought you had the measure of somebody, they do something completely unexpected and totally pull the rug out from under your feet. You may have to go back to the drawing board where this relationship is concerned because it appears that you've made some wrong assumptions and now you don't know where you stand with this person.

• *Thursday 4 May* •

How are your finances at the moment? If you are a typical Libran, this is the sort of question that has you clutching your head and humming a tune to block out such an unpleasant thought. However, today's New Moon is reminding you that it's time to take a long, hard look at all your money matters. Maybe you should get a new savings scheme off the ground or perhaps you need to ask the advice of a financial expert? Once you set the ball rolling it may not be nearly as gruelling as you feared.

• *Friday 5 May* •

You are filled with wanderlust today and if you've planned to get away this weekend you'll have the time of your life. Your ideal destination is somewhere that offers lots of cultural and educational stimulus because you would be bored stiff lying on a beach or sitting by the pool all day. If you are staying put at home, how about giving your brain an airing by visiting a gallery or museum?

• *Saturday 6 May* •

You are in a very sympathetic mood today and the chances are that someone will seek you out for advice on a very personal matter. Your intuition is working well, and no matter how hidden the problem seems to be, you will go straight to the heart of it and identify a possible solution. Where an intimate partner is concerned, you'll know what they're thinking before they even say anything.

• *Sunday 7 May* •

One-to-one relationships are of the utmost importance to you today and you'll want to concentrate on improving them and achieving a greater sense of well-being and harmony. You feel well-disposed towards everyone you meet, and your genuine warmth and affection for loved ones will go a long way towards establishing greater cooperation between you. You may not realize it but you hold the key to creating a happier state of affairs.

• Monday 8 May •

If there is someone in your life who is older and wiser than you, and who acts like a mentor to you, this would be a good time to get in touch with them. Perhaps there is something that you would like to discuss with them? You've been so busy propping everyone else up recently that you have neglected yourself in the process. Someone at work could give you a helping hand in some way.

• Tuesday 9 May •

You are in rather a soul-searching mood today and you'll want time to yourself to process your various thoughts and feelings. Perhaps a recent heart-to-heart has given you food for thought and made you question yourself and your relationships? If your patience has been pushed as far as it can go by a certain person's behaviour, now is the time to put a stop to it.

• Wednesday 10 May •

This is an ideal day to push yourself forward and take centre stage. There seems very little that can dent your confidence at the moment and anything that you start today is set to do well. You are ready to push yourself higher up the ladder and you've got all the motivation you need to help you to achieve your ambitions. It promises to be a highly satisfying and productive day.

• *Thursday 11 May* •

Expect the unexpected today, especially when it comes to certain people in your life. Someone that you thought you knew inside out could take you by surprise when they reveal a totally new aspect to their personality. There could also be a dispute over someone's emotional freedom. If you are the one who wants a more committed or conventional relationship than your partner, you may have to give them their head for the time being.

• *Friday 12 May* •

Partnerships of all kinds go from strength to strength today, especially if both parties are able to be completely honest with each other. You're entering a period of consolidation and you will feel very secure and reassured by the noises that others are making. If you've got a chance to potter around the house or garden for a couple of hours, you'll unwind nicely in time for the weekend.

• *Saturday 13 May* •

Today has the makings of one of the best days in the year because one of your dreams could come true. Something you've been hoping and yearning for is about to materialize. This could involve a trip abroad to a very special place, an academic achievement or a career opportunity. Anything, in fact, that allows you to be creative and to broaden your horizons. If all goes well, you will want to celebrate in style, so spoil yourself and open a bottle of something nice.

• *Sunday 14 May* •

You will be very talkative and communicative over the next two weeks, making lots of phone calls and sharing your news with everyone. If there are some ideas that you want to discuss, get them out in the open and see what the general response is. Think big because you can make great strides now and open doors that you didn't even know existed before.

• *Monday 15 May* •

You can leave a lot of emotional baggage behind today and make a fresh start in some way. If you've been holding on to an attitude or belief about yourself that is no longer true, you now have the courage to let it go and replace it with a much more positive sense of who you are. If you feel confident to go it alone, you'll feel a sense of liberation from doing so. This will be a very exhilarating and stimulating day.

• *Tuesday 16 May* •

There is a very highly charged atmosphere between you and a certain person today. It could even culminate in a very passionate encounter. Part of the reason for your mutual attraction at the moment is the fact that you have been so honest and open with one another recently. Take care when handling money matters because there could be a misunderstanding with someone. It will be better to be safe than sorry.

• *Wednesday 17 May* •

Good fortune shines on you today, especially where your finances are concerned. If you've been trying for some time to get yourself on an even keel and keep within a budget, you will feel justifiably pleased with yourself now about how much more in control you are of your spending. You could even receive a windfall or some kind of pay-out which will boost your security even further.

• *Thursday 18 May* •

If you find yourself getting in a state about nothing, it's probably because today's Full Moon is making you extra sensitive and emotional. As long as you're aware that you're liable to turn every molehill into a mountain and that you have temporarily lost your sense of proportion, things won't get too out of hand. Allow yourself a couple of treats to make you feel better.

• Friday 19 May •

You're ready to learn something new about the world today and you'll have the chance to embark on a voyage of physical, mental or spiritual exploration. Whatever level your journey is on, it will enrich your life no end and give you a new and exciting perspective. If you come across a subject that stimulates your interest, don't hesitate to find out more – it will open up all sorts of new horizons.

• Saturday 20 May •

This is one of those days when you have to take a deep breath and just let the words you want to say come out. Whatever it is that you have on your mind, you feel extremely strongly about it and the only thing that's holding you back from saying it is fear of getting into somebody's bad books. Have the courage of your convictions.

• Sunday 21 May •

Although you can achieve a lot today, take care not to be foolhardy and to avoid overextending yourself completely. You might do something that is physically demanding, and while there's nothing wrong in pushing yourself that bit harder than usual, you should try to respect your limits otherwise you are likely to do yourself an injury. You may find that having lots of short breaks helps to extend your stamina.

• *Monday 22 May* •

Don't be too pliable today because a loved one or someone at work could try to talk you into something that may not be in your best interests. However good their intentions might be, for some reason they believe they know best where you're concerned so you will have to speak up loud and clear if you want them to register your protest.

• *Tuesday 23 May* •

The rigours of your daily routine may feel somewhat restricting today, yet you will have to resign yourself to staying on the treadmill if you want to get everything done. Look on the bright side and acknowledge that the more structure that you have in your life at the moment, the more productive you can be and the more rewards you will reap. Don't give up!

• *Wednesday 24 May* •

Thank goodness you can have a more sociable day today! Even though there are still certain commitments that you have to honour, you can at least spend some of the time in the company of good friends. You will feel as though you haven't had a good chat in ages and you will probably bend the ear of at least one unsuspecting person. It's called making up for lost time!

• *Thursday 25 May* •

If you're a Libran who has a love of travel and adventure, the next few weeks promise to bring you lots of beneficial and pleasurable experiences. If you're going abroad you could have a wonderful holiday romance, or you might fall in love with the place and wonder whether you should live there. If you are staying at home, you could lose your heart to an interest or study that makes your world a better place. The possibilities are endless!

• *Friday 26 May* •

The question of how well you look after yourself crops up again today and you get another chance to refine your diet or give up a health-damaging habit. If you feel that you're not coping with stress very well at the moment and that you have one or two symptoms which support that idea, it's not too late to do something about it. Talk to someone who's in the know about such matters.

• *Saturday 27 May* •

You could meet someone really fascinating today and you will feel as though your brain has had a work-out merely from talking to them. Being in stimulating company is your idea of heaven now, and if you happen to be attracted to the person you're talking to, then you will need for nothing else. You could hear out of the blue from a long-lost friend or relative. What a day!

• *Sunday 28 May* •

You could receive a proposal today that will ambush you completely. A certain someone may pop the question, or you could be given an offer by a friend or loved one that appeals to you in a completely different way. Whatever the situation, you won't beat about the bush in giving your answer because you will intuitively know exactly what you want. You may look back on this day as a turning point in your life.

• *Monday 29 May* •

It will take a lot to faze you today because you're feeling very relaxed and content. You probably don't have a preconceived idea of what you want to do today, which is fine because you'll be quite happy to take it as it comes and make the best of whatever situation you find yourself in. Your good mood is contagious and people will feel happy and relaxed in your company. One person you meet may seem too good to be true, but are they?

• *Tuesday 30 May* •

Your compassionate side is aroused today and you'll want to put some of your time and energy into helping others in some way. This could take the form of working for a cause or charity that is dedicated to making the world a better place, or you might lend a hand to a friend in need. You'll have all the energy you need for whatever is important to you at the moment.

• *Wednesday 31 May* •

It is very difficult to understand a certain person today and you may give up on them completely. They could say one thing and do another, or they may be sending out so many mixed signals that you feel you ought to be communicating in semaphore because then you might stand a better chance of knowing what they are on about. Keep love and money as far apart as possible, otherwise there could be disappointments – or worse.

JUNE AT A GLANCE

Love	❤ ❤
Money	£ $
Career	💻 💻 💻 💻 💻
Health	☼

• Thursday 1 June •

Your emotions are highly charged today, making you react quite strongly to situations. Although you might normally laugh some things off you will take them much more seriously now, and while that may be positive in some circumstances, where your love life is concerned you could get yourself into a bit of a state. On the plus side, your intensity could drive you to achieve more than usual.

• Friday 2 June •

Good news! Today's New Moon offers you some exciting insights over the coming fortnight about the direction in which your life is heading and you will now be able to make plans for the future. Seeing the bigger picture is enormously helpful at this time and it will add meaning and purpose to what you are doing. You will also receive confirmation that you are thinking along the right lines.

• Saturday 3 June •

Do you have anything special planned for the weekend? Apart from your busy social calendar, your interest in subjects connected with mind, body and spirit could take you to a talk or festival where you will learn a lot more and meet some like-minded people. If you are ready to study something in more depth, now's the time to explore the various possibilities.

• *Sunday 4 June* •

Talk about being decisive! Putting your cards on the table and saying exactly what you think will be a piece of cake today, and you will be able to sort out any resentments or misunderstandings between you and a certain person. You feel very clear about the current state of your emotions and whatever you say will come out exactly as you intend it to.

• *Monday 5 June* •

A work colleague does something today that really touches you and makes you see them in a completely different light. Perhaps they're particularly sensitive to your mood and act in a protective way towards you, or they might give you the benefit of the doubt when others may have been less accommodating. Showing your appreciation will forge a bond between you.

• *Tuesday 6 June* •

Friends are terrific company today, and you could be fascinated by what you hear from one chum in particular. They might tell you something that makes you view life in a new way or they could bring you a lovely opportunity. It's also a great day for studying subjects that interest you, especially if they have philosophical, spiritual or religious overtones.

• *Wednesday 7 June* •

You will have no problems in summoning up the enthusiasm for whatever is on your agenda today. Provided that you can devote yourself to a project or task that you find rewarding and fulfilling, you will be happy to put in as much time as necessary and you won't even feel drained by all that hard work. You can also enjoy a laugh with someone who always lifts your spirits.

• *Thursday 8 June* •

You are looking to improve your life today, and if you have to convince someone that you're worth more than they think, you will certainly put across some very forceful arguments. A sibling or relative may have been taking you for granted and you might now have suddenly woken up to the way they've been treating you, or a boss may have been overlooking your talents. Not for much longer!

• *Friday 9 June* •

Try to temper your words with a little caution today, especially if you're talking to someone who could easily be upset or offended. By the same token, you could make the mistake of thinking that somebody has it in for you and become ultra-defensive as a result. You might have a serious discussion with somebody close to home that has a depressing effect on you and makes you want to retreat into your shell.

• *Saturday 10 June* •

You might need to spare some time for a loved one today and be their shoulder to cry on. They might simply be feeling under the weather and need cheering up, but there may be something more serious that they're worried about and which they will want to confide in you. Fortunately, you're full of sympathy and understanding and are only too willing to give them some TLC.

• *Sunday 11 June* •

You have been undergoing some big changes recently and this is a good day to evaluate how far you've come, and what and who you want in your life. Taking a good look at yourself isn't always easy as it can stir up unwanted thoughts and feelings, but your sense of equilibrium right now means that you've got what it takes to take a dispassionate look at your current circumstances.

• Monday 12 June •

If you are working as part of a team today, the spirit of harmony and cooperation will prevail and everyone will do their best. If you've been locked in a power struggle in the past with one particular colleague, you will find that the friction between you has now dissipated. If you take the initiative and offer the olive branch, you will establish a much more positive relationship between you.

• Tuesday 13 June •

You will really appreciate a change of scene today, and you'll find it mentally refreshing to meet new people, especially if they're different in some way from what you're used to. If your social life needs jazzing up, think about casting your net far and wide and seeing what (and who) is beyond your own backyard. It's time to open up your horizons!

• Wednesday 14 June •

Your confidence is riding high today so it's a fabulous opportunity to pursue any personal projects that you want to get off the ground. You can initiate lots of new things in your life at this time, both in your personal and professional worlds. All you really need is conviction in what you're doing and a strong belief in yourself. It's as simple as that.

• Thursday 15 June •

Is your nose twitching? Whatever you do, don't dismiss your hunches today because you'll have an uncanny knack of getting them right. Call it a sixth sense or simply intuition, but the important thing is that you can use it to help you get to the truth of a matter or read between the lines of what someone is saying. Don't analyse, simply trust in the messages you receive.

• *Friday 16 June* •

You could easily feel restless or trapped today, and rather irritable as a result. The Full Moon doesn't help – in fact, it's part of the reason you're champing at the bit. You may feel fed up with your current routine and in need of a change of scene, in which case you need to think how you can make this happen. Even small changes to your daily schedule will make you feel rejuvenated and revitalized, so don't imagine that it's got to be all or nothing.

• *Saturday 17 June* •

There's a lot to do on the home front today and you'll want to get everything shipshape, especially if you're having friends over and doing some entertaining. A loved one may need careful handling, especially if they get in a flap about something or threaten to burst into tears given the slightest provocation. Let off steam by doing something energetic or creative.

• *Sunday 18 June* •

For the next few weeks you will be giving a lot of thought to how well you earn your living and whether your work offers you enough scope to express all of your abilities. Your ambition is fuelled at the moment so if you're not happy with the status quo you need to introduce some changes that will give you greater freedom of expression. Set aside some time today to get your plan of action together.

• *Monday 19 June* •

If an old skeleton threatens to rattle the cupboard door today, don't see it as something negative. Instead, welcome the opportunity to face up to an old fear and finally let it go. This could be something from your past that you thought you had dealt with but which suddenly re-emerges from out of the blue. You are better equipped to handle this than you think and, besides, look at how much support you've got.

• *Tuesday 20 June* •

Who's in seventh heaven? Get set for a sexy day full of romance and affection. It could also be exciting when eyes meet across a crowded room. You could be introduced to someone through work who's just your type, and the chemistry between you almost threatens a meltdown. On the other hand, a well-established relationship could be about to experience a renaissance – and how!

• *Wednesday 21 June* •

You could receive an invitation today that fills you with excitement and keeps you in a permanent state of anticipation. There's no point in trying to play it cool because it's obvious to all and sundry that you're hot to trot! If you're going out tonight on that nail-biting first date, before you go out of the door check your hair for static! It's probably standing on end with excitement!

• *Thursday 22 June* •

The last thing you want today is to be left alone for long. You're feeling far too sociable for that and you're probably bursting to talk to a good friend about some exciting new developments. Even if you thought you would jinx things by talking about you-know-who too soon, it would take a super-human effort for you to keep quiet at the moment. Don't fight it!

• Friday 23 June •

You have been such a live wire recently that it won't be surprising if you suddenly run out of steam today and feel that you need to take it easy for a while. If you've got the chance to pamper yourself and give yourself some nice treats, you'll soon feel revitalized and ready for the next round. You might even fancy a night in front of the TV with your feet up. Why not?

• Saturday 24 June •

Do you fancy giving yourself a treat? Then buy something that will improve your health or give a big boost to your ego. If you have fallen out with a colleague or partner recently, you will be able to jolly them out of their bad mood now. Do something that makes them laugh or be prepared to talk about what went wrong and how you can stop it happening again.

• Sunday 25 June •

If you are experiencing some wear and tear in your emotional fabric today, make sure that you protect yourself from any unnecessary slights or barbed comments. You are more sensitive than usual at the moment and, although you're more than capable of looking after yourself, there's no point in putting yourself in the firing line. Choose the company you keep wisely.

• Monday 26 June •

You are raring to go today and you're brimming with ideas and plans that you want to put into action. Before you go rushing off to conquer the world, you might need to consider what a partner or loved one wants to do and whether they can fit in with what you're doing. It's fine if they are perfectly happy for you to do your own thing, but if not, you might need to do a little cajoling.

• *Tuesday 27 June* •

You're in a very constructive mood today and ready to sort out any difficulties that might have taken place recently with a partner. It probably isn't anything very serious and you should easily come up with a simple solution that you can both feel happy about. You might have to do some trouble-shooting at work, so be prepared to roll up your sleeves.

• *Wednesday 28 June* •

You could be expected to do more than your fair share of work today, but if you can accept it with a good grace and not kick up a fuss, you'll be doing yourself and everyone else a big favour. It's not that you're being exploited, it's more a case of all hands on deck in order to meet a deadline. Your efforts won't go unnoticed or unappreciated.

• *Thursday 29 June* •

There could be a contretemps today with a colleague or associate and you will need to use all your diplomatic skills to prevent a rift forming between you. Goodness knows what's got into them, but they seem to be spoiling for a fight and trying to get you to rise to the bait. They could simply be offloading their anger on to you because you're a convenient scapegoat. The outcome depends on you.

• *Friday 30 June* •

There are countless opportunities coming your way over the next few months and some fabulous new experiences are beckoning. The big question is – are you ready and willing to take a step to meet your destiny? Your curiosity and desire for positive change will propel you forward, and any slight trepidation that you feel won't be enough to hold you back. Good luck!

JULY AT A GLANCE

Love	❤ ❤
Money	£ $
Career	💻 💻 💻 💻
Health	☼

• Saturday 1 July •

You will be feeling very single-minded during the coming fortnight and you won't be easily deterred from doing what you want to do. You will want to put as much time and effort as you can into furthering your goals and ambitions, and because you're such a powerhouse of energy at the moment, there won't be many stones that you leave unturned. Be as enterprising as you can and you'll reap the rewards.

• Sunday 2 July •

You can look forward to a meeting of minds today, when you'll be thrilled to discover how much common ground you share with a certain person. You'll feel so comfortable chatting and exchanging ideas that you could easily find yourself confiding in them and revealing sides of yourself that you normally keep under wraps. Sounds like a good basis for a friendship – or possibly something more?

• *Monday 3 July* •

This is a great day to show off any creative skills you have and to acquire a higher profile. You're able to reach great heights now in your career, provided you have faith in your abilities and don't undersell yourself. If you feel that promoting yourself isn't your strong suit, get an expert to help you write your CV or give you some careers advice. Once you see on paper what it is that you have to offer, it could boost your confidence no end.

• *Tuesday 4 July* •

Don't worry if you had a slightly wobbly patch yesterday because you'll more than make up for it today. You have the energy and determination to put yourself forward, and you now realize beyond a shadow of a doubt that you can't stand still and just wait for something to happen. The more positive your intentions are, the more likely you are to succeed.

• *Wednesday 5 July* •

You feel very passionate and emotional about a goal that you've set your heart on and you'll discover today that you're one step closer to making it happen. This will put you in a very decisive frame of mind and renew your sense of purpose. In fact, so keen are you to get on with the job in hand that it's likely to be your main focus until you've clinched the deal. Are you committed or what!

• *Thursday 6 July* •

Keep tabs on your ideas because you could come up with a brainwave about how to handle a work situation that's been bothering you recently. Your thoughts are coming fast and furious and you've got so many lightbulbs going off in your head that unless you write some of these gems down, they'll be gone with the wind. It might be politic to keep quiet about any changes that you plan to make until you're 100 per cent sure.

● *Friday 7 July* ●

Have you been cooped up in one place for too long? If so, you will need to get out today and breathe some fresh air. If you feel that you need to spread your wings, why not take some time off this weekend and give yourself a much deserved break? Do you remember the saying 'a change is as good as a rest'? That's exactly what you'll get if you put everything on hold for a couple of days.

● *Saturday 8 July* ●

You'll get a big kick out of doing something different today, especially if it involves being in a new environment with lots of places to visit. If you can't get away, make sure you spend time with friends doing something really enjoyable. One friend in particular will play an influential role in your life in the coming days – and they'll come up trumps in an unexpected way.

● *Sunday 9 July* ●

You're on top form today and socially you can expect to have a ball. You're exuding that famous Libran charm again and, needless to say, someone is going to be captivated by you. It's not that you're feeling particularly flirtatious – in fact, you're more in the mood for serious conversation than light-hearted banter. Give anyone who's unduly negative a wide berth.

● *Monday 10 July* ●

Busy? You bet you are, but the good news is that you'll be totally absorbed by what you're doing and the time will fly by.

The question of finances could come up and if you've been meaning to spend some time sorting things out, this is an excellent day to go through your statements and bills and get up to date. You will feel a lot more in control when you know where you stand.

• *Tuesday 11 July* •

You will invest a lot of emotional energy in something that you consider to be very important today. Someone close to home could need your support, in which case you'll be willing to drop everything to be by their side. Alternatively, there could be a situation at work that needs your full attention and you will have to focus on that to the exclusion of everything else.

• *Wednesday 12 July* •

Unless there's something to pull you back, you will drift off into a world of your own today and quite happily spend the time mulling over your passing thoughts. It's a wonderful day for getting together with some of your favourite people, especially if you don't do anything very energetic but simply enjoy one another's company. It's a great excuse to go out for a drink or a meal.

• *Thursday 13 July* •

Are you all set for a fabulous three weeks, full of love and laughter? You'll find any excuse for a party or get-together between now and early August, and you and your best friends will take great delight in spending time with each other. If you're a sporty Libran, you will enjoy doing something athletic, especially if it involves an element of competition. You're going for gold in everything you do now.

• *Friday 14 July* •

Life is hectic today and you will need to pace yourself if you want to keep your cool. You could be in a situation where all eyes are on you and you have to come up with a creative solution or innovative idea. You won't have any problem rising to the challenge and you'll secretly bask in all the attention – in spite of the stress involved.

• *Saturday 15 July* •

For the next few weeks you will be able to introduce a very positive influence to any group activities that you're involved in or organizations that you belong to. Your social life will also be highlighted and you will enjoy making the most of this time by getting out and meeting people and making new friends. Cultural activities will hold a special appeal, so get ready to expand your world.

• *Sunday 16 July* •

Your true self comes out during the next two weeks, and you will be able to enjoy being yourself with friends and family alike. You will be in rather a sentimental mood and you'll have no hesitation in expressing your warm feelings for those you love and cherish. If you've been taking a certain someone for granted recently and leaning rather heavily on them, you'll want to let them know how much you care for them and appreciate them.

• *Monday 17 July* •

What's in charge today – your head or your heart? It looks as though your heart will win the battle, and this may explain why you're feeling rather emotional and finding it hard to keep a lid on certain emotions. Enjoy the fact that you're feeling so open and communicative and if you do feel a strong emotion take hold, let it run its course rather than see it as a threat.

• *Tuesday 18 July* •

You stand a good chance of success today if you're hoping to talk someone into helping you in some way. It's also a marvellous day for being sociable and relaxed with people who don't expect you to be anything other than your true self. A loved one could spring a surprise on you or do something that makes you reappraise your opinion of them. You may have to struggle to keep your sense of humour about this, but you will manage it!

• *Wednesday 19 July* •

Are you ready to eat humble pie? If you stepped out of line with someone recently but for some reason didn't apologize to them, you will have the perfect opportunity today to make amends. It's also an excellent day for tying up any loose ends, especially if you're going on holiday soon and you've got a deadline to meet. It may seem as though it's all work and no play, but you'll soon redress the balance.

• *Thursday 20 July* •

You could discover that something or someone is holding you back in some way today. As a result, you have got to shift this blockage and move forward. Whatever or whoever it is no longer has a place in your life and no matter how much you try to hang on to it, sooner or later you will have to come to terms with the fact that it is time to move on. It's time to make up your mind.

• *Friday 21 July* •

This will be a red-letter day where your love life is concerned and you'll thank your lucky stars about how everything turns out today. Are you about to tie the knot, or is a certain someone going to give you a call? Either way, you're as sure of your feelings as you ever will be and in no doubt about your willingness to make a commitment. Happy days!

• Saturday 22 July •

You're in an impulsive and impetuous mood today but be careful not to rush in where angels fear to tread or you could come out with egg on your face. Try to temper your enthusiasm with some self-restraint and then you will stay on the right side of people. If you feel that your sense of humour is slightly too wicked for everyone's taste, bite your lip and scale it down!

• Sunday 23 July •

You will have to watch your step today because feelings run high and emotions are volatile – if not explosive! Be especially careful not to arouse someone's jealousy because they could go completely OTT and upset everyone. In your book you could just be having some innocent fun, but such behaviour might be totally misinterpreted and make you very unpopular.

• Monday 24 July •

You might as well take it easy today because you won't have the energy to motivate yourself to do much. You're in rather an indolent and self-indulgent mood but, rather than feel guilty about it, why not give yourself permission simply to do nothing. Think of it as time to recharge your batteries for the week ahead. Hit the snooze button and relax!

• Tuesday 25 July •

Expressing your thoughts and ideas will be second nature to you today and you will want to talk to as many people as possible about the subjects and topics that interest you. This would also be a wonderful time to go to a talk or lecture and listen to someone else's ideas, especially if there's a chance for you to ask questions at the end. You will be fascinated.

• *Wednesday 26 July* •

This is a fabulous day for thinking about your general well-being and vowing to break any bad habits that are damaging your health. If you've been feeling under par recently, spring into action by starting a new regime or having a health assessment with a professional to get you on the right track. Just think of all the extra energy you'll have as a result!

• *Thursday 27 July* •

If you decided to take yourself in hand yesterday you will already be feeling better – even if it's only psychologically at this stage. You exude confidence and energy now and, with your new-found resolve, you'll be full of high hopes for becoming a fitter, healthier you. Just be careful not to get too carried away and do yourself more harm than good – Rome wasn't built in a day.

• *Friday 28 July* •

You could be smitten by someone new today and have a wonderful time discovering all there is to know about one another. It doesn't necessarily have the makings of a long-term relationship but you'll make quite an impact on each other and it will change the way you see yourself and the world. It will be fleeting but memorable – and it sounds exciting!

• *Saturday 29 July* •

You've got bags of stamina today and the more physical you are the better you'll feel. This would be an ideal day to take a long hike, or to test your powers of endurance in some way by pushing yourself to the limit. If you still don't feel fit enough to challenge yourself that much, start on a smaller scale and gradually work your way up.

● *Sunday 30 July* ●

You are not feeling very organized today and it will take you longer than usual to tackle any jobs or chores that need doing. If you're at work, try to delegate as much as possible so that the onus isn't entirely on you. If you're lucky enough to be on holiday, securing your space by the pool might be the most challenging task you have to meet. Relax and take life easy whenever you get the chance!

● *Monday 31 July* ●

It's a marvellous day for making plans, and the bigger they are the better. You can make some very positive changes during the next few days that will make more room in your life for the things you really enjoy. If you're a true Libran, you're always trying to get the balance right, and this is one of those rare times when you can do just that. Congratulations!

AUGUST AT A GLANCE

Love	♥ ♥
Money	£ $
Career	💻 💻 💻
Health	☼ ☼ ☼

● *Tuesday 1 August* ●

It's a very energetic start to the month, and during the next six weeks you will channel lots of energy into making your ideas a reality and thereby fulfilling some ambitions. You will be able to work at your very best and not only motivate yourself but inspire others to cooperate with you to make this happen. Being a team leader is your natural role at the moment, and you will be able to do it with both open-mindedness and authority.

• Wednesday 2 August •

Your current optimistic mood will help you to push things forward today, but it's important that you don't get carried away to the point where you forget some important details. You will have to keep an eye on every aspect of whatever project it is you're working on and, if you're signing any papers, don't forget to read the small print. A friend or neighbour could be rather forceful.

• Thursday 3 August •

You might think that you're cooling off where a certain relationship is concerned, but it's more likely that you need some time alone to consult your feelings and come to terms with what's being stirred up emotionally in you. Needing to withdraw could be your way of taking stock, so try not to make any important decisions until you have thought them through carefully.

• Friday 4 August •

You are very sensitive to the feelings of others today and you'll probably get involved in helping at least one close friend with an emotional problem. This might be a welcome distraction from your own unresolved emotional dilemmas and you will be more than happy to focus on someone else's difficulties. However, don't use this as an excuse to sweep your own feelings under the carpet.

• *Saturday 5 August* •

You'll be in no doubt about a partner's loyalty and support today, and this will give you the green light to take the initiative and put your relationship on a stronger footing. Perhaps you've been waiting all along for a sign that you're truly appreciated and loved, and now that you have it you'll no longer want to hold yourself back.

• *Sunday 6 August* •

You could learn a valuable lesson today about your emotional patterns and how they affect your relationships. If you feel that you need constant reassurance and you can't trust yourself to show your feelings spontaneously, it might be worth thinking about the reasons behind your fears. Nothing is cast in stone, and as long as you're prepared to work on yourself you can change whatever you aren't happy with.

• *Monday 7 August* •

It's one of those days when you have no idea what's going to happen next and you simply need to go with the flow. Plans could be changed at the last minute or someone you thought was reliable may turn out to be a bit of a space cadet. Give yourself plenty of leeway to make other arrangements if necessary, and try to be as philosophical as you can about the disappointments.

• *Tuesday 8 August* •

If your life were a canvas you would want to be painting in broad, colourful brushstrokes right now and to be as free and creative as possible. Unfortunately, reality is somewhat different today and you could feel as though you're having to paint by numbers with no room for your imagination whatsoever. Try to find some kind of middle ground – at least for the time being.

• *Wednesday 9 August* •

You're champing at the bit today and longing to explore pastures new. If you're about to go on holiday or you've already taken off, then this is a day to expand your horizons. You'll want to take in as much as you can and if you're going sightseeing you will be totally captivated by the beauty of the places you visit. Memories are made of this!

• *Thursday 10 August* •

Who's feeling rebellious today? A loved one or family member could be in a bit of a strop today and, unless you nip it in the bud, their behaviour is likely to make everyone's life a misery. If a group of you are planning an outing and this person is the one dissenting voice, try talking to them to see why they're being so contrary. Be prepared for a few unexpected developments later in the day.

• *Friday 11 August* •

As long as you don't bite off more than you can chew today it looks as though you're all set for a wonderfully sociable day with lots of your favourite people. If you've taken it upon yourself to organize a get-together, the logistics may turn out to be a bit of a nightmare, so before you get to the end of your tether, enlist some practical help. Many hands make light work.

• *Saturday 12 August* •

Your mind is razor sharp today and you'll be in your element if you have to do anything that involves intense concentration. If you're playing a game of tennis or cards, you'll easily be able to outsmart your opponent and leave them scratching their head in bewilderment. Similarly, if you engage in some kind of debate you'll gain the upper hand through your mental alacrity. Clever you!

• *Sunday 13 August* •

You exemplify the benefits of positive thinking today because anything that you turn your hand to will work out well. You can challenge yourself to take on more than you would normally, knowing that you have the capability to extend yourself and come up trumps. Provided that you're aware of your personal limits and don't overreach yourself, you will be even more productive and effective than usual.

• *Monday 14 August* •

You and a certain person are striking sparks off each other today and this will create a lot of tension between you. You might have an almighty row and end up between the sheets for a passionate reconciliation. If you need to discuss where your relationship is heading, wait for another time when you've cooled down a bit and are feeling less volatile. Otherwise, you could say the wrong thing.

• *Tuesday 15 August* •

A friend or sibling could drop a bombshell over the next two weeks and leave you speechless. Whatever their news, it will be the last thing you expect from them and it will take quite a lot of getting used to. Be careful that you don't go OTT and alienate them as a result. You might not be happy with the situation, but you'll only make it worse if you overreact.

• *Wednesday 16 August* •

You've got stacks of nervous energy today and you will need to find some positive outlet for it if you want to avoid ending up with a splitting headache or a feeling of exhaustion. Try to take your mind off whatever is bothering you and do something therapeutic to relax and absorb you. If you get the chance to have a massage, you'll definitely unwind!

• *Thursday 17 August* •

It's important to keep an open mind today and not be so preoccupied with your own point of view that you exclude other opinions. Taking the time to understand someone a little better will improve your relationship no end and make you more tolerant of each other. However, it does all depend on you taking the first step, so you may have to swallow your pride.

• *Friday 18 August* •

You might decide to arrange a surprise party for someone today or fix up some other form of treat for this person. You will want to show your appreciation for all that they've done for you and you won't want to spare any expense. If you're thinking of buying them a gift and you're not sure what to get them, why not take them on a shopping trip and let them choose. That way you can't go wrong.

• *Saturday 19 August* •

This isn't a good day to enter into any kind of negotiations, especially if they're legal or binding, and you'd be wise to postpone matters until Tuesday when the odds look more in your favour. The problems lies in the fact that you'd be willing to take a risk, but without properly weighing up the situation first. Whatever you do, get the right help before you sign on the dotted line or make a commitment.

• *Sunday 20 August* •

You probably feel in the need for some light relief today and you won't be disappointed because there are all kinds of invitations for you to choose from. Leave any worries behind you and let your frivolous and playful side have a run for its money. If it's a while since you've had some pure, unadulterated fun, this is your cue to let your hair down and enjoy yourself.

● *Monday 21 August* ●

You are in an extravagant mood today but, before you splash out, make sure that there is enough money in the kitty to pay for whatever you've got your eye on. It could be that you've got less than you thought, and even though you were counting on making certain purchases today, you might need to wait until you're back in the black. It's called delayed gratification!

● *Tuesday 22 August* ●

A conversation with someone from a different culture or walk of life gives you plenty of food for thought today and you might decide to follow up a suggestion they make. This could involve you in deviating from your normal path and exploring something totally new, but you're intrigued and in the mood to investigate. You will be fascinated!

● *Wednesday 23 August* ●

Are you ready to have your confidence in yourself tested? It's important to be true to yourself today and not allow what others think of you to worry you unduly. You may have a decision to take that is something of a moral dilemma and it could make you very unpopular with a certain individual. Talk it over with someone you trust and respect, and whose support you can count on.

● *Thursday 24 August* ●

You could come across some fascinating reading matter today that totally transports you to another time and place. Your mind will so enjoy travelling on such a wonderful journey that you might decide to visit one of the places described, or learn a new language. There are so many options available to you that you'll feel spoilt for choice. What a luxury!

• Friday 25 August •

You're in the mood to spoil and nurture those you love, and if you're a dab hand in the kitchen you might decide to create a culinary masterpiece and entertain everyone at home. If you're a classic Libran, you'll want to add lots of pretty touches and have everything absolutely perfect. You might even think of a theme and get everyone to dress up for the occasion.

• Saturday 26 August •

You're still feeling very warm and affectionate towards loved ones and close partners, and you won't mind one bit if you have to put yourself out for one of them. You'll gain a tremendous amount of satisfaction from giving your all and knowing that you make a difference in people's lives. You couldn't ask for more at the moment.

• Sunday 27 August •

They say that what goes around comes around, and today you'll certainly be surrounded by people who are willing to give you their full support and backing for whatever you want to do. Will you stand by them when their turn comes? You might be considering a change of job or a house move, and the fact that no one is opposed to any of your plans gives you a free hand to go ahead.

• Monday 28 August •

If you're deciding what to do today, plump for something totally different from the norm. You would be bored stiff if you did anything vaguely routine or familiar, so be as experimental as possible and choose the wacky option. If you feel like doing something that is really hair-raising, why not get a crowd together and go to an adventure park or a dry ski-slope? Have fun!

• *Tuesday 29 August* •

Today's New Moon puts you in a quiet and reflective mood and you might feel like escaping from the world for a while during the next two weeks. Thoughts and feelings that float to the surface will need to be integrated and accepted by you, and you may need a period of time to come to terms with this new part of you. Listening to music or going for long walks will help you put things in perspective.

• *Wednesday 30 August* •

This is another low-key day when you feel like being with one or two close friends and not doing anything very demanding. Going to the cinema, watching a video or eating out are all good ways of taking it easy now. If you are at work today, it may take you a while to get into the swing of things. Ease yourself in gently.

• *Thursday 31 August* •

If you've got a long list of jobs to do today, you will need to organize yourself so that you have the time to get everything done. Structure your day as much as possible and be strict with yourself about how many breaks you take. You'll feel a lot happier once you've broken the back of your workload, and you'll enjoy your free time all the more if you know that you have done your best.

SEPTEMBER AT A GLANCE

Love	♥ ♥ ♥ ♥ ♥
Money	£ $ £
Career	💻 💻 💻 💻
Health	☼ ☼ ☼ ☼ ☼

• *Friday 1 September* •

Take a good look in the mirror today, then have a glance at your wardrobe. Do you like what you see? If you feel bored or fed up with your current image, the next three weeks are the perfect time to change it in some way. Treat yourself to some new clothes, ask your hairdresser to transform your looks or do something else that will make you smile every time you see your reflection.

• *Saturday 2 September* •

If you usually pride yourself on being a good judge of character, be very wary today because you could get your fingers burnt. If you meet someone who makes a strong impression on you and dazzles you with their charisma, remember that all that glitters isn't gold. So before you get set to ride off into the sunset with them, check out what's behind the façade. If you are going to be disappointed, it will be better to know sooner rather than later.

• *Sunday 3 September* •

You've got real pulling power today and you can attract almost anyone you set your sights on. If you're currently single and you've been waiting in vain for a certain someone to make the first move, you'll be delighted to know that your waiting days are over. Whether they were plucking up the courage to approach you or just biding their time, they're now good and ready. It will also be a red-letter day for an existing partnership. You're going to be busy!

• *Monday 4 September* •

Are you tiptoeing on eggshells around someone? Whoever is being so edgy and defensive has made you so intimidated that you're afraid to say the wrong thing and set them off. Best to give them a wide berth while they're in such a bad mood, but you'll need to stand up for yourself and do some straight talking with them at some point if you don't want history to repeat itself.

• *Tuesday 5 September* •

If your job involves communication, publishing, buying, selling or education, you're all set to have a bumper day. You'll excel at whatever you do and not only will you receive lots of praise and recognition for doing a good job, you could also pull in a large amount of money. Although it may not all be for you, if you are lucky you will be able to keep a hefty portion of it.

• *Wednesday 6 September* •

What a shame it's the middle of the week because you're all set to party the night away. Whether or not you've got something to celebrate, you're in the mood to enjoy yourself and you'll use all your powers of persuasion to entice a few friends out for a night on the town. There are bound to be a few die-hards who'll be willing to burn the candle at both ends, so it looks as though you will go to the ball after all.

• *Thursday 7 September* •

Are you ready for a quantum leap forward? The next three weeks will bring many opportunities for advancement in all areas of your life and you'll be able to fulfil a dream or ambition that means a great deal to you. If you believe in yourself and show the world what you're made of, providence will do the rest. All the cards are stacked in your favour at the moment, and all you have to do is play them right.

• *Friday 8 September* •

Your feelings run very deep today and you'll want to spend lots of time with your intimate partner, preferably between the sheets! Your emotional intensity is so strong that you won't be able to think very logically, so you will really be up against it if you find yourself in a situation where you have to be rational and objective. Use your intuition as a back-up.

• *Saturday 9 September* •

The best way to get to know someone today is to talk to them and encourage them to open up and say how they feel. By the same token, you will need to be equally honest about your own feelings because it will be through sharing them that you really establish a close bond. If you have a child who's been behaving rather badly recently, it will help to use the same tactics with them.

• *Sunday 10 September* •

Your love life flourishes today and you will revel in the company of some of your favourite people. If you need to say something to clear the air between you and a certain person, you will be able to do it without being heavy-handed and hurting anyone's feelings. If possible, go out for the day and allow your carefree side out to play – you'll have more fun than you can imagine.

• *Monday 11 September* •

You are more concerned with getting ahead today than putting your energies into other people, and you're feeling very single-minded about what you need to do for yourself. If someone accuses you of being selfish and only thinking about yourself, don't take it too much to heart. Whatever their agenda might be, you know that there are times when you have to look after number one.

• *Tuesday 12 September* •

An opportunity may come your way today that won't announce itself with a big fanfare and so could easily be missed if you're looking the other way. It could come in many subtle guises, so you'll need to stay very open-minded and not dismiss anything out of hand. Even when you do think you've identified it, you may have to wait a while before it reveals its full potential.

• *Wednesday 13 September* •

The next two weeks are a great time to assess your progress so far and re-evaluate where you want to go from here. You're in a remarkably positive and optimistic mood now, and no doubt you'll feel as if everything is going to plan. In fact, you may even be doing better than you'd hoped. You really deserve to give yourself a pat on the back for everything you've achieved so far.

• *Thursday 14 September* •

If you recently started a platonic relationship with someone, don't be surprised if one of you suddenly starts to feel a more sexual attraction. This may complicate things no end and you'll have to think very carefully about the implications of starting a romance with this person. One thing's for sure, staying 'just good friends' will no longer be an option.

• *Friday 15 September* •

You are a real tower of strength today! Someone who looks up to you could come to you today in need of some financial or practical help. You'll gladly do whatever you can, and even if you're not in a position to give them a loan, you'll be able to offer all kinds of advice and support to help them resolve their difficulties. You will have a very productive day at work and feel good about what you're doing.

• *Saturday 16 September* •

You've got a list as long as your arm of things that you want to do this weekend and you'll probably be up at the crack of dawn to get an early start. If you've recently started a new course of study, you may have an assignment to do or some reading to catch up on. A group or organization that you belong to could be holding a meeting which you need to attend. All in all, you'll be very busy.

• *Sunday 17 September* •

During the next few weeks you may experience feelings of anger that you didn't even know you had. Unless you own it and accept it, you could find yourself on the receiving end of other people's rage and frustration. Be careful too that you don't end up fighting someone else's battles for them as you'll only end up the loser. It may not be easy to come to terms with such a strong emotion, but in the long run your relationships will be smoother if you do.

• *Monday 18 September* •

Certain attitudes and beliefs of yours are undergoing changes at the moment and you're starting to look at yourself differently. You might even surprise yourself, not to mention everyone else, with some of the new concepts that you come up with! You could well become a guiding light or mentor for someone who's still grappling in the dark with who they are.

• *Tuesday 19 September* •

You're in a wonderful state of balance today, with both your intellect and your intuition working in tandem. You're not overwhelmed by your emotions, neither are you being overly logical, and the fact that you find yourself somewhere in the middle gives you a tremendous sense of well-being. And it's not only you who will feel the benefits – anyone who comes into your orbit will feel uplifted by you.

• *Wednesday 20 September* •

You're in a rather daring mood today and you'll feel much more courageous about saying what you think and standing up to people who normally intimidate you. Suddenly the fears you've had about rocking the boat no longer have such a strong hold on you and you feel free enough to express your true self. Watch out, world!

• *Thursday 21 September* •

You could feel rather tense today, especially if certain people seem to be ranged against you or they are conspicuous by their absence. Try not to let your frustration escalate because it will only slow you down and create yet more stress. Concentrate on things that you can do well and let the rest take care of itself – you can only do your best.

• *Friday 22 September* •

You start to experience an enhanced sense of your own self-worth today and your confidence begins to soar. Over the next four weeks there will be glorious times when you feel that you are fulfilling your destiny and making the most of your life. It's a marvellous time to launch a new venture or get a project off the ground, or you might simply enjoy being you and discovering new facets of your personality.

• *Saturday 23 September* •

This is a good day to reconsider some of the commitments you have made and to ask yourself whether any of them are beginning to feel as though they are untenable or no longer valid. It's not that you don't want to honour the agreements you've made, but if you feel as though you're carrying more than you can comfortably handle, then you need to talk to the people concerned and see what can be done to alter the situation.

• *Sunday 24 September* •

If you are feeling any uncertainty over what to do about a loved one or partner, you can safely bet that honesty will be the best policy today. You may be reluctant to hurt their feelings by coming clean, but they're probably much better equipped to deal with the truth than you think. Have you considered that you may be blowing the whole thing way out of proportion?

• *Monday 25 September* •

You may be confused about a loved one's motives today and start to behave suspiciously as a result. What you might not have considered is the possibility that they themselves are relatively clueless at the moment about why they're behaving in a certain way. Give them the benefit of the doubt and try to broach the subject without any blame or recriminations.

• *Tuesday 26 September* •

If you've been longing for something wonderful to happen but didn't dare hope it would, you'll be happy to know that today promises to fulfil your expectations. This could be a very private aspiration that means the world to you but that you haven't shared with anyone in case of disappointment. Once you receive confirmation that it is going ahead, however, everyone's going to know about it.

• *Wednesday 27 September* •

The accent is on your finances for the next few weeks and you'll be looking at ways to invest your money and build a nest egg for yourself. If you haven't managed your economy very well in the past, you're about to wise up fast and you may even decide to take a crash course to increase your knowledge. This will put you in the driving seat and make you feel much more in charge of your life.

• *Thursday 28 September* •

The rapport between you and a certain someone deepens today and you'll almost feel at one with them. This will feel very emotionally gratifying and you'll enjoy the closeness and intimacy that you share. If you've been skirting around the edge and flirting with the idea of taking the plunge, this could be the day when you make that special commitment and go for broke.

• *Friday 29 September* •

You will be the life and soul of any party you go to today and if you have you-know-who by your side, you'll also be the star of the show. All sorts of people will flock to your side and be reluctant to let you out of their sight. You'll just have to put up with being the centre of attention all evening – what a penance!

• *Saturday 30 September* •

Stand by for some good news about a financial arrangement today. It will mean that you can start making plans for the future. You're probably more in the mood for a quiet day, although you won't want to be completely on your own. You might feel like phoning a friend and asking them over for a cosy chat, or suggesting to your partner that you cook a meal together and stay in.

OCTOBER AT A GLANCE

Love	♥ ♥				
Money	£	$	£	$	£
Career	💼	💼	💼		
Health	☼	☼	☼		

• *Sunday 1 October* •

You are full of goodwill today and you'll want to spread as much happiness as you can to those around you. It's almost as though you've got an endless supply of joy inside and no matter how much you give out, it just seems to replenish itself. If you're getting together with anyone who is unwell or down in the dumps, they will benefit enormously from your company.

• *Monday 2 October* •

Your self-confidence gets a big boost today and you'll be striving to gain greater recognition for yourself in some way. You could be headhunted for a new job or a boss who's been rather mean in their praise may suddenly tell you how good you are. Rather than simply rest on your laurels, you will feel inspired to go on to greater things. There's no stopping you now!

• *Tuesday 3 October* •

You need a mentally challenging situation today to keep you on your toes and stretch you to your full potential. If your work is connected with selling, advertising or travel, there will be lots of exciting developments to keep you fully occupied. In your personal life, a love affair will suddenly feel a lot more intoxicating than usual.

• *Wednesday 4 October* •

You will feel like a free spirit today and you won't want to be tied down or stuck in a routine. You're able to excel now and if you're in a competitive situation you will really pull the stops out to win. Proving yourself is important to you and you'll rise to any occasion that provides you with the opportunity to reach your personal best. Talk about dynamic!

• *Thursday 5 October* •

Are you in a rather introspective mood? You're feeling very self-contained and self-sufficient today and you'll happily be able to work for long periods on your own. You're able to depend on yourself and know that you're strong enough to handle life's ups and downs, but not afraid to ask for help if you need support. Whatever is familiar will feel very comforting, especially your everyday rituals.

• *Friday 6 October* •

Yesterday's realizations have stimulated a powerful urge in you to become more of your own person and less willing to compromise. You'll feel very motivated to address any situation in your life where you feel you're being a bit mealy-mouthed and not being true to yourself. Whoever has got used to you being that way had better fasten their seat belt because they're in for a shock.

• *Saturday 7 October* •

Are you ready for a journey into the unknown? If you're feeling restless, this is the perfect weekend to take a short break away somewhere and recharge your batteries. Without having a specific destination in mind, a group of you might decide to jump in the car and see where you end up. The more spontaneous you can be, the more fun you'll have.

• *Sunday 8 October* •

If you are currently in a relationship but away from home today, you could be tempted to stray by an exciting stranger that you meet. You might also be entranced by someone that you meet closer to home, and once again you will have to decide whether to flirt with them or whether to do the honourable thing and keep well away. This person could be very tempting and you may have to battle with your conscience.

• *Monday 9 October* •

You could be acting out of character today so that a loved one or partner will wonder what's got into you. You may not be any the wiser yourself – all you know is that something inside you is changing and it hasn't quite taken shape yet. You will feel somewhat irritable if anyone tries to corner you and find out what's wrong, so give yourself plenty of space.

• *Tuesday 10 October* •

You're much more in tune today with how you're feeling and you'll no longer need to keep others in the dark as to the mystery of your recent behaviour. Communication is the key to building a bridge of understanding between you and a certain someone, and once you've done that you'll no longer feel as though you're a million miles apart.

• *Wednesday 11 October* •

You may have to defend your ideas in the face of opposition today, but you'll do it in an intelligent and good-humoured way and you'll have no difficulty in getting your point of view across. You're thinking big and you want others to share your vision and grandiose ideas. They may be resistant at first, but your enthusiasm alone will eventually convert them.

• *Thursday 12 October* •

You really are flavour of the month at the moment and everyone has a good word to say about you. Someone may want to pick your brains about one of your ideas and you could have an extremely fruitful and productive conversation with them. You might put a suggestion to a boss or superior that they reject at first, but they'll soon see that there's method in your madness.

• *Friday 13 October* •

Not only is it Friday the 13th, but there is also a Full Moon. Are you carrying a lucky rabbit's foot, just in case something awful happens? Your relationships will be highlighted over the next two weeks, and if you need to set matters to rights or give someone a piece of your mind, things could become worse before they get better. But don't lose sight of the bigger picture, nor of your conviction that you are entitled to have your say.

• *Saturday 14 October* •

Do you feel like spoiling yourself today? You won't need any excuse to visit your favourite shops and buy yourself some-thing sexy and glamorous, or something that boosts your confidence. You are definitely in the mood to treat yourself to some luxuries, and you might also splash out for your partner as well. Even so, go carefully when handling finances because money will flow like water. Not good news if you are already facing a drought!

• Sunday 15 October •

You will enjoy your domestic routine today, especially if you have lots of close relatives over for Sunday lunch. You'll enjoy the warmth and closeness of family ties and you'll get a lot of pleasure out of cooking something delicious for everyone and making them feel loved and welcome. A walk in a beautiful setting would be the perfect ending to a wonderful day.

• Monday 16 October •

You're in a brilliant mood today and your high spirits will colour even the most mundane chores. If you've been putting a lot of energy into making your world bigger and better, you'll begin to feel the positive effects of all your efforts and will feel encouraged to go one step further. You could make some very useful connections that open yet another door for you.

• Tuesday 17 October •

There's a surprise connected to something that you've been looking forward to and you might have to make some last-minute changes to your existing plans. Someone that you've been longing to see may turn up earlier than you expected, and you'll want to drop everything so that you can spend some time with them. You could also hear from someone out of the blue.

• Wednesday 18 October •

If you have to attend a rather formal gathering today, you'll do a good job of breaking the ice and putting everyone at their ease. This is a situation where your Libran diplomatic skills and innate charm come into their own. Even though you may take such talents for granted, your host will be more than appreciative of your ability to create such a convivial atmosphere.

• *Thursday 19 October* •

If you're currently counting the calories and getting rather cheesed off by the whole thing, give yourself a day off today and enjoy a meal with friends and family. There's no point in stinting yourself because you're in the mood for having whatever you fancy, and that in itself will do you good. If you're really determined to continue watching your weight, you can resume your regime tomorrow.

• *Friday 20 October* •

If you're trying to make headway today and you seem to be beset by nothing but irritating delays and setbacks, you won't have much choice but to bite the bullet and wait until everything starts to flow again. To add insult to injury, someone could let you down or renege on an agreement at a crucial moment and you'll be left holding the baby. These things are sent to try us.

• *Saturday 21 October* •

You are blessed with the gift of the gab over the next few weeks and your words will have quite an impact. If you teach or have to speak in public, you'll come across with great fluency and you'll enjoy passing on your knowledge or giving out information. If you've had any difficulties with a close member of the family, you will be able to find a way forward and resolve your differences.

• *Sunday 22 October* •

If you have had a fantasy of a dream lover and never thought they existed in real life, watch this space because they could appear before your very eyes today. The only catch is that they may not be available and you might have to look but not touch. Don't despair, however, because if there is an attraction between you, something may develop at a later date.

• *Monday 23 October* •

For some reason you feel the need to keep your emotions on a tight rein today and give away as little as possible. This could be because it's not the time or the place to show how you really feel, or you might feel too vulnerable if you open yourself up. Try not to withdraw completely or shut down your feelings because such tactics will only make you feel worse.

• *Tuesday 24 October* •

Someone close to home could be acting distant or aloof today and it will be hard to know if they're reacting to your mood or whether something else is bothering them. It could be that your relationship has reached an impasse and it's make or break time. Alternatively, your partner may be distracted by something that has nothing to do with you. Only by talking things through will you get an idea of where you stand and what is wrong.

• *Wednesday 25 October* •

You need to consider your long-term plans today. If you come to the conclusion that any of them are no longer relevant or valid, you will need to pluck up the courage to leave them by the wayside. Only things that support your growth and your true self are worth preserving, and if you have outgrown something you will simply shed it like an old skin.

• *Thursday 26 October* •

What's bothering you? You're in a rather vulnerable state today and you feel like retreating into your shell and keeping the world at bay. If you're licking your wounds after a rather emotional time with a certain someone, you're doing the right thing by stepping back and assessing the damage. Time is the great healer and you will need to be patient. In the meantime, be kind to yourself.

• *Friday 27 October* •

Thank goodness today's New Moon offers you a chance to draw on your inner strength and make a fresh start. Whether you're starting a brand new chapter or beginning an entire new book, you can leave outworn situations behind you now, knowing that there's a rhyme and reason to what's transpired and that it is time to move on. You are much stronger than you think. Onwards and upwards!

• *Saturday 28 October* •

This is a wonderful day to take stock of recent developments and come to terms with how you're feeling at the moment. You can learn a lot if you look back to other relationships in your life and understand what they taught you. As you grow and change, so do your needs, and it's important that you re-evaluate exactly what it is that you now need and want from life.

• *Sunday 29 October* •

You are in the mood to talk to people today about whatever is vitally important to you. Fortunately, you've got lots of friends and loved ones who are only too happy to act as sounding boards, so you'll get a lot of valuable feedback. This is one of those times when you appreciate the wonderful support that you have and you realize how rich you are in love and friendship.

• *Monday 30 October* •

There's no point in trying to keep the peace today because you'll only anger the person you're doing your best to placate. You might as well both let your true feelings out, even if that means having a shouting match, because at least that way you can let off steam and clear the air. You'll be surprised how quickly you can kiss and make up afterwards. You might even decide to make it a regular part of your relationship!

• *Tuesday 31 October* •

If you managed to express any pent-up feelings yesterday you should be feeling a lot stronger today. If you decide to persevere with a situation that you still believe has potential, make sure that you have the emotional stamina to stay the course and that you're not setting yourself up for another fall. Don't be surprised if your self-confidence hangs in the balance for a while.

NOVEMBER AT A GLANCE

Love	♥ ♥ ♥
Money	£ $ £ $
Career	💻 💻 💻
Health	☼ ☼

• *Wednesday 1 November* •

Family and domestic matters take precedence today and you'll need to focus on resolving a minor upset. If you have children, one of them may need your sympathy and understanding. Whatever you do, avoid being heavy-handed with loved ones because, even though you think you should be firm, most of all they need some TLC.

• *Thursday 2 November* •

You're in a much perkier mood today and you'll enjoy meeting lots of people and being sociable. You're determined to have some light-hearted fun, and if you're a solo Libran you'll enjoy a brief flirtation with someone new. For you this could simply be an exercise in proving to yourself that your powers of attraction are as strong as ever, so be careful not to give the wrong message.

• *Friday 3 November* •

Although you're probably quite busy at the moment and don't have a lot of free time, it would be a good idea to arrange a few treats between now and the end of the year. Doing something just for you will give you the balance you need and prevent you from getting too stressed or overtired by all the other things in your life. With one of the busiest times of the year coming up, you certainly need to pace yourself.

• *Saturday 4 November* •

It might seem a little early for Christmas shopping but if you've got a vague idea of the presents you want to buy, this would be an ideal time to get at least some of them crossed off the list. The more organized you are at this stage the better, especially if you're planning to have people to stay over the festive season. You know what they say about the early bird . . .

• *Sunday 5 November* •

You're in very businesslike mood today and you'll get a lot of work done around the house as well as any other jobs that are pending. Your no-nonsense attitude won't go down so well with a certain person who may want a more relaxing time, but no doubt you'll manage to persuade them to muck in. If you're going to a fireworks party, guess who'll be the one to organize everything?

• *Monday 6 November* •

Using your brain will give you enormous satisfaction today and you'll jump at the chance to resolve a problem or come up with a creative solution. Your thinking is very intuitive and the ideas will flow without any great effort on your part. You'll know instinctively how to communicate with others, and if you have to thrash something out you will be both receptive and assertive.

• *Tuesday 7 November* •

This is a wonderful day to do something creative or imaginative, especially if it involves a project connected with work. Your mind isn't operating in a logical or analytical way and this will work to your advantage because you will be able to think in an inventive and original fashion. If a close relative or a neighbour calls on you for help, you'll know exactly how to respond.

• *Wednesday 8 November* •

Be very careful today because this is a bad time to take risks, especially if you can't afford to lose. For instance, if someone tries to sell you an insurance policy or a financial package, make sure you can trust them and double-check all the details because you could easily be duped. By all means look into ways of making your money grow, but be wary of get-rich-quick schemes.

• *Thursday 9 November* •

Clearing your life of anything that no longer fulfils a purpose has been an ongoing process for you recently, and today you may find that you come across something else that you're now ready to jettison. If your home still contains a lot of clutter, or some of your personal belongings have seen better days, do yourself a favour and let them go.

• *Friday 10 November* •

You can't help but say what's in your heart today and you'll disarm a certain someone with your candour and direct approach. This will turn out to be in your favour because the feelings you have will be more than reciprocated, giving you a wonderful sense of comfort and security. Your libido is at a peak at the moment so there will be lots of sexy moments to look forward to!

• *Saturday 11 November* •

The image that you present to the world and the way you really are may be two different things, and you might sometimes feel as though you are not expressing the real you.

Today's Full Moon urges you to show a more authentic personality to the world and to allow whatever is deep within you to be more visible. You will find that there is tremendous power and strength to be gained by tapping into your true self. You could surprise yourself!

• Sunday 12 November •

'Live and let live' is your best motto today, and it is the one that will give you the greatest opportunity to enjoy the day. It may be that someone is acting out of character and you don't know the best way to handle them. Leave them be and focus on your own life, because the more you try to change them, the more they'll resist. Get together with someone with whom you don't have to make any effort.

• Monday 13 November •

You're feeling much more laid-back and relaxed from today and far less concerned about the behaviour of others. In fact, you will have nothing to worry about on that score because your social life is going to give you plenty to smile about over the next few weeks. You could receive lots of enticing invitations, just in time for the party season. It sounds as though you may have to buy some new clothes so you're all set to dazzle everyone in sight!

• Tuesday 14 November •

If you're at work, try to delegate as much as possible because you're liable to bite off more than you can chew and become totally fraught as a result. A colleague or assistant may be more on the ball than you are today, and although they could prove themselves to be invaluable, you may not be able to trust them completely. Could they have a hidden agenda that you're not aware of?

• Wednesday 15 November •

Make sure you spend the time with people who are in the same kind of easy-going mood as you today. You're feeling especially good about yourself at the moment and if you've been working hard on getting yourself fit and healthy, you'll be extra pleased with the shape you're in. Any kind of social activity that includes some of your favourite people is highly recommended.

• Thursday 16 November •

You're starting the run up to the Christmas celebrations and you'll be concentrating on getting things organized today. If you're planning on having house guests over the festive season, there will be plenty of work to do around the home, and you'll want to do as much as you can in good time. And while you're at it, why not draw up your Christmas card list?

• Friday 17 November •

You'll be the star turn today, whether you're at a social gathering or at a work function. If you're trying to drum up business, you'll have potential clients eating out of your hand. Your popularity is assured! You'll have no qualms about using your charms to dazzle whoever you're talking to and gain the advantage. As they say, if you've got it, flaunt it!

• Saturday 18 November •

If you are wise you will avoid mixing money and pleasure today, because they don't go together. However, even if you manage to avoid mixing them, a certain person may not be so clever and could stir up trouble by asking you to do something that you are not prepared to tackle. Watch out for someone who feels jealous or possessive and can't help showing it.

• Sunday 19 November •

You are very aware of your actions and how they affect others today. Being more responsible for the way you relate to your nearest and dearest and how you handle your emotions will have an extremely positive effect. It could make you review your relationships and it could also help you to deal with a tricky situation that develops and which needs careful handling.

• Monday 20 November •

The past few days have been rather intense but you get the chance to have a breather today. Thank goodness for that! It's a wonderful excuse to spend time with someone you care about, especially if it's just the two of you and the rest of the world doesn't have to intrude. You could be asked to listen to someone's tale of woe or you might need to offload some of your own thoughts on to someone's broad shoulders.

• Tuesday 21 November •

Any ideas that you come up with today will pack a terrific punch and you'll be able to talk your way into anything with the minimum of effort. If someone has been entrenched in their position up until now, you'll be able to penetrate their defences. You might even manage to give the impression that they should take all the glory for this change of heart, even though you engineered the entire thing.

• Wednesday 22 November •

You'll have no difficulty in fighting your corner today, and to say that you have the courage of your convictions would be an understatement. You totally believe in yourself and in what you're doing, and anyone who is foolhardy enough to try to persuade you otherwise will soon get cut down to size. This is one occasion when keeping the peace is not a priority.

• *Thursday 23 November* •

Activities connected with further learning and travel are well aspected today and you might be thinking about studying something new or taking a break over the holidays. Expanding your mental and physical horizons will be an extremely liberating and intoxicating experience, and also a welcome change from your everyday routine.

• *Friday 24 November* •

Someone once said that if you look at a person's past, it will tell you about their future, and this may be something you might want to consider today. Looking at the way that the past has shaped you will give you lots of clues and insights into the way that you behave, and how this can influence what happens to you in your life. You could gain some valuable insights if you think about this in depth.

• *Saturday 25 November* •

With the run-up to Christmas you'll be much more involved in your domestic circumstances than usual over the next fortnight, and there will be a lot of list-making and shopping to do. In spite of the fact that you may already have done quite a lot already, you're beginning to feel the strain and you will need to pace yourself to avoid getting into a state. Take lots of deep breaths!

• *Sunday 26 November* •

You could have a conversation with a close relative today that helps you to understand one another better. You might reminisce about the past and talk about all sorts of things that make you both laugh and cry. If you need to ask a neighbour for a favour, they will be more than happy that you asked and you'll realize that you can help each other out in lots of ways.

• Monday 27 November •

Set aside some time for a hobby or favourite activity today because it will not only relax you but it will boost your energy levels no end. No matter how busy you are, try to set aside a little time for yourself. Social settings will call to you like sirens, so grab the chance to go out with someone if possible. Even a trip to the shops with a friend will make you feel good and be a lot of fun.

• Tuesday 28 November •

Life is for living today, and you are fully prepared to roll up your sleeves and get stuck in. Ideally, you should don your favourite clothes and go in search of the jazziest and loudest party you can find. Someone dear to your heart could endear themselves to you even more than usual, especially if they make you laugh or remind you of how special they are. If you are doing some Christmas shopping you will carry home some wonderful trophies, some of which may be for you!

• Wednesday 29 November •

You're feeling very emotionally strong and secure at the moment, which is probably why someone who needs a shoulder to cry on comes to you today. There's no danger of you absorbing their mood, but you're sensitive enough to appreciate how they feel and you'll do your best to console them. If you're in charge at work, people will respect you and look up to you.

• *Thursday 30 November* •

You feel calmly composed today and you'll take anything that comes along in your stride. You can take a realistic view of your life and feel good about the way things are going, rather than wishing it were all different. A member of the family may earn your compassion or care, or you might take great delight in honouring a family tradition that makes you feel part of a bigger picture.

DECEMBER AT A GLANCE

Love	♥ ♥ ♥ ♥ ♥
Money	£ $
Career	💻 💻
Health	☼ ☼

• *Friday 1 December* •

This may not be a very seasonal thought but you need to spend time today thinking about the current state of your finances. If you still have a long list of presents and other things to buy before the festivities can begin, you really need to take stock of your expenses this month. Can you afford them easily or will you have to rob Peter to pay Paul? Perhaps you need to have a quiet word with your bank manager . . .?

• *Saturday 2 December* •

If you're a Libran with a highly idealistic streak, you will be very aware of this side of you today because you will expect the best from people. Sometimes this can backfire on you and you end up feeling disappointed, but this time you will be glad to know that a lot of your expectations will be met. Family life and relationships in general all look set to improve no end.

• *Sunday 3 December* •

A highly charged current of energy is flowing between you and a certain person today. Exciting as that may be, it will also make you feel extremely jumpy. Is this an attraction that you can do something about or do you have to keep it under wraps? Either way, you're feeling a strong pull towards this person that will be hard to resist.

• *Monday 4 December* •

You want to live life to the full today and one relationship in particular will make you feel very alive. Your communication with others is both intense and rewarding now, and you will want to talk about matters that are very close to your heart. You could throw caution to the wind and declare your feelings for someone, in which case there will be some interesting developments in the coming weeks.

• *Tuesday 5 December* •

Even if you have to surmount a few problems today you'll make the best of the situation and view any difficulties as a chance to learn from experience. If someone is in a bad mood and spoiling for a fight, you'll handle them with patience and forbearance, and you might even put yourself in their shoes to see why they're so annoyed. Needless to say, this brilliant strategy will work a treat!

• *Wednesday 6 December* •

This would be a wonderful day to curl up with a good book and escape the world for 24 hours. If that's totally unrealistic and you have a million other more pressing things to do, try to make time at the end of the day for at least a little time to yourself. With the festive season just around the corner, finding a few private moments each day could be your saving grace.

• *Thursday 7 December* •

You may be surrounded by chaos today but don't panic because you'll be able to maintain an oasis of calm inside yourself. If you've been practising yoga or meditation, it will be useful to have a few relaxation techniques up your sleeve. If not, you can still manage to stay cool under pressure while everyone else is having a meltdown. Call it mind over matter!

• *Friday 8 December* •

Just in time for the festivities, your popularity starts to shoot through the roof. During the rest of December you will be in great demand, not only as a party guest but also as someone who is loved and cherished by lots of people. If you are currently a Libran on the loose, you could soon be snapped up by someone smart who knows a good thing when they see it. If you are already spoken for, your other half will make a massive fuss of you. Ain't life grand?

• *Saturday 9 December* •

Try to take things gently today and do something that doesn't take up too much energy. You will enjoy all the festive preparations as long as you don't push yourself to do too much. If there are a few extra-special presents that you still have to get, you'll almost certainly find what you're looking for, even though it means spending a bit more than you had budgeted for. And why not?

• *Sunday 10 December* •

If you're planning a big family celebration this Christmas, you'll really want to push the boat out and make it an occasion to remember. The next couple of weeks look pretty hectic, so today could be the last time that you can actually go at your own pace and spend time choosing the decorations and little touches that will give your home that extra sparkle.

• Monday 11 December •

During the coming fortnight you may have to wrestle with your conscience about something that challenges your philosophy of life or your moral code. This may take some grappling with, especially when you realize that things aren't as cut and dried as you first thought. You may also have to deal with someone's prejudice or narrow mind, and this will need careful handling.

• Tuesday 12 December •

If someone is being particularly difficult today and challenging everything you do, they won't leave you with much choice but to confront them and point out to them how badly they're behaving. Whatever pressure they're under, there really isn't any excuse to behave like a spoilt two-year-old. Without being overly threatening, you should let them know in no uncertain terms that they'd better sort themselves out – or else!

• Wednesday 13 December •

Take care today, especially when handling people who are old enough or wise enough to know better. They might throw their weight around or issue orders as though you are a skivvy. You could also encounter someone who is fiercely ambitious and who raises doubts in your mind. Is this person trying to use you as a stepping stone for higher things and will they dispose of your services as soon as it suits them?

• Thursday 14 December •

You are feeling unashamedly sentimental today, and what you'll most enjoy is being with your loved ones and telling them how much they mean to you. You'll especially feel like cuddling up close with someone special and whispering sweet nothings in their ear. If you start to feel really nostalgic about the past, it will do you good to talk about it with people who share your history. Expect laughter and tears.

• *Friday 15 December* •

You will instinctively know how to bring out the best in people today, which means that good fun will be had by all. If you have got some pent-up energy and you want to find a positive way to release it, try to make time for a swim or a long walk. If time is of the essence and you can't even squeeze half an hour of exercise into your busy schedule, you can always count on some laughter therapy to do the trick.

• *Saturday 16 December* •

Can't make up your mind? You're pulled in two directions today and unless you make a decision you're likely to drive yourself – and everyone else – mad. Part of you feels you should concentrate on getting any last-minute jobs out of the way before the big countdown, and another part of you just wants to go out and strut your stuff. Is there any way you can see to get the most important jobs done and then go wild? You'll find a way.

• *Sunday 17 December* •

Friends and loved ones make the world go round today and any social occasion spent in their company promises to be extremely enjoyable. If you're a typical Libran you do love a compliment, so you'll be glad to know that someone will make your day by saying something that makes you feel like a million dollars. Flattery will get them anywhere!

• *Monday 18 December* •

Telling you that love is all around you today must be music to your ears, and exactly what you wanted to hear. All your relationships, whether romantic, platonic or business, are well starred now and you will mix with ease with anyone you come into contact with. Your creative gifts are also in the ascendant, so try to express them whenever you get the chance.

• *Tuesday 19 December* •

The wonderful part about being with people you feel close to and comfortable with is the fact that you don't have to pretend to be something you're not. Being yourself, and knowing that others love you for it, is very important to you right now. No wonder you're feeling so happy! It's a very good day for having a heart-to-heart with someone special, especially if you feel safe enough with them to be completely honest and open.

• *Wednesday 20 December* •

If you're prepared for this to be one of your busiest days, you're less likely to be fazed by the workload you are facing. If you're at work, there will be a frantic rush to get everything done in time and you won't have a minute to spare. On the home front, there are still chores galore to see to but, if you're systematic about it, you'll be able to take everything in your stride.

• *Thursday 21 December* •

If you've lost track of how much money you've spent recently, it might be a good idea to sit down and go through your accounts today, so you can get a rough idea of how your finances are looking. That's probably the last thing you feel like doing, but the sooner you take control, the more secure you will feel. If you need to discuss your feelings with someone, do it today while you're in the mood.

• *Friday 22 December* •

You're feeling very sensual and passionate today and you'll want to spend a romantic evening with a certain sexy someone. If you've had your eye on you-know-who and you're just beginning to sense that the attraction is mutual, one of you might make your move today. After all, what's the point of fantasizing when you can have the real thing?

• *Saturday 23 December* •

Although you're now in the throes of the festive season, there will be times during the next few weeks when you need to think about your personal and domestic life and whether you need to make any changes. Discussions with family members will bring a lot of things to light as you'll be able to voice your innermost thoughts and feelings. Something from the past may need to be cleared up before you can go any further.

• *Sunday 24 December* •

Your desires for everything that you value in life are starting to intensify, and they will continue to be uppermost in your mind until next February. During this time you will be actively going out to get what you want. You will want to enjoy all the things that money can buy, and if you don't feel that you have enough cash you'll be pursuing different ways of increasing your financial status. It's time to grow stronger and more resourceful.

• Monday 25 December •

Happy Christmas! You're all set for a wonderful day, despite the fact that you will probably be extremely busy. Fortunately, you're feeling much more energetic than usual so you won't mind if the onus is on you to do most of the work. There will still be plenty of time for you to enjoy some fun and games, and you'll particularly enjoy talking to a family member who will have you in stitches.

• Tuesday 26 December •

You are in a more serious and reflective mood today and this would be the ideal time to think about any New Year's resolutions that you want to make. If you really do want to turn over a new leaf and let go of a part of your life that is played out, or to stop a bad habit like smoking, you'll have more willpower than you think. All you have to do is make up your mind.

• Wednesday 27 December •

You will really enjoy being at home today and taking things easy. You're not in the mood to make any kind of effort and you'll probably feel like watching TV or reading a book. If you could have some time to yourself that would be even better, because then you will be able to completely switch off and relax. You could always sneak off for an afternoon nap!

• Thursday 28 December •

If you need to get something off your chest today, take the initiative and say how you feel. You'll be surprised at how easy it is to get your point of view across and how receptive the other person is to what you have to say. If you're dealing with a work-related matter, it's important that you state your position now so that there's no ambiguity about where you stand.

● *Friday 29 December* ●

You feel like doing something completely different today, and if you have the chance to take off for a day or two it will do wonders for you. You want to get as far away as possible from domesticity and routine, and if you have a group of friends who are on the same wavelength as you and who feel the same, what's to stop you from giving yourselves a short break?

● *Saturday 30 December* ●

You feel the need for strong emotional contact with others today and you'll want to be with people who have a strong rapport with you. It's a wonderful time to grow closer to a partner and to establish a deeper connection with them, especially if you've felt disconnected recently. The boundaries between you seem less definite so you stand a better chance of really understanding one another.

● *Sunday 31 December* ●

There is no need to ask if you're ready to greet the New Year because the answer is obviously yes! You're positively glowing today and, with your love life blooming and other areas of your life starting to open up, you've got a lot to look forward to. You're entering 2001 on a high note, so go all out to enjoy yourself tonight and make it a fabulous start to a fabulous year.